31 London Cemeteries to Visit Before You Die

31 London Cemeteries to Visit Before You Die

TERRY PHILPOT

step
beach

First published in Great Britain in 2013 by Step Beach Press Ltd, Brighton

A CIP catalogue record for this title is available from the British Library.

ISBN 978-1-908779-03-8

Typeset in Turners Hill, UK by Christine Gardner
Cover design by Christine Gardner. Cover photos ©Nagib ©Godrick Shutterstock
Photographs by Stephanie Dale

Printed in Singapore. Manufactured and managed by Star Standard Industries Pte Ltd.

Step Beach Press, 28 Osborne Villas, Hove, East Sussex BN3 2RE

www.stepbeachpress.co.uk

To my dear friend, John Dossett-Davies (1927–2009), possessor of all kinds of arcane knowledge, which would have made him the ideal companion to have walked these paths with me.

Contents

Acknowledgements

Many people have helped to shape this book. My first thanks must go to Chris Parker, Director of Step Beach Press, who had an idea that he mentioned casually to me, and which we then turned into this volume. I must also thank Jan Alcoe, Chris's fellow Step Beach Press Director, for her interest and support. Suzi Baker took some of the excellent photographs, while Steph Dale researched the photographs. Vicki Williams, as copy editor, made useful suggestions. Robert Philpot meticulously read most of the manuscript, picked up several repetitions, errors and stylistic infelicities, and made a number of helpful suggestions that improved what I had written.

Jennifer Gerber explained differences within Judaism, and Mohamed Omer, board member of the Gardens of Peace Muslim Cemetery Trust, explained Muslim burial practice. Richard Baldwin, business administration manager, London Borough of Islington, answered questions regarding Finchley Cemetery. Rev Edwin Quildan, minister of the Fetter Lane Congregation, took time to show me around the Moravian burial ground, while Lorraine Parsons, archivist for the Church's British province, answered several detailed questions. Gordon Wolffe offered a highly informative, often amusing guided tour of Highgate Cemetery (West). The Sunday afternoon tour of Kensal Green Cemetery, given by Henry Vivian-Neal, author of the indispensable *Paths of Glory*, a guide to those buried there, was rich with anecdotes and information. He also kindly read, improved and corrected that cemetery's entry. I am also grateful to the Friends of Tower Hamlets Cemetery Park for their help; to Paul Weigand, researcher with the Abney Park Trust, who clarified some details; as did Ron Woollacott, Chairman of the Friends of Nunhead Cemetery (and himself author of highly informative guides to the cemetery). JRL Schneider of the Church of St Mary-le-Savoy gave me information about the German church's history. The staff of the British Library were, as always, helpful and efficient.

Introduction

Many years ago I stood by a hillside cemetery in Trinidad, where graves were often marked only by rough, wooden crosses, and some had flowers placed in pasteurised milk cans. On another occasion, I stood in awe of the serried ranks of simple, white headstones stretching out as far as the eye can see in the cemeteries where Allied troops, casualties of the Normandy landings, are buried in Northern France. In the Capuchin catacombs of Palermo, Sicily, one walks the arched aisles, along each side of which the mummified dead stand in rows, dressed in the fashion of the day: priests and monks in clerical garb; others wearing the dress of country people, born high or low. In Washington DC, the graves of the Kennedy brothers are shielded by an eternal flame, while below and above them run the dignified, immaculately kept graves of the American war dead, stretching back to Revolutionary times.

Great lives commemorated contrast, poignantly, with how unknown ones are sometimes mourned. However the dead are remembered – from the most humble to the most exalted, from the most powerful to the most dispossessed – is shown in the cemetery, churchyard or burial place. 'Sceptre and crown must tumble down/And in the earth be equal made with the poor crooked scythe and the spade' says James Shirley in his drama, *The Contention of Ajax and Ulysses*, seeing death as the great equaliser.

Death may be the great equaliser, but the churchyard, burial place and cemetery also shows that even in death, there is often no equality in how we are remembered. Compare, for example, the extravagant memorials of Highgate or Nunhead with the common graves of Tower Hamlets. The delights of the English churchyard, running up to ancient stone walls, shadowed by oak trees, is deep in our culture – and, indeed, for many, our daily experience if we are fortunate to live close by to such places. But we overlook the barely marked graves of, for example, the Irishmen who lived in London's hostels and rest now in Finchley Cemetery.

However, there is more to a cemetery than who is buried there and I hope that this book reflects that. Not everyone interred may be significant, but their tombs may be of interest. The cemetery's location, its history, its atmosphere, its buildings may give it a status that its inhabitants do not confer. As this book is not intended to be a comprehensive guide, I have had to select those places that tend to combine an interest in who is buried there with an interest in other features of the site.

I have defined a burial place – a term that includes both cemeteries and churchyards – as somewhere whose prime function, whether still operating as such or not, is the burial of the dead. This, then, rules out the most of the former London churchyards that are now largely public gardens, often with headstones pushed against peripheral walls, occasionally with a tomb to be seen.

Which burial places to include and which to leave out was not an easy task. The great Victorian cemeteries (among them, the Magnificent Seven) exist with the dozens of other municipal cemeteries, and other burial places.

A cemeterey's age alone does not guarantee its inclusion. For example, I have omitted Paddington (Willesden Lane) Cemetery (1855) because, attractive though it undoubtedly is (and if one happened to be walking by it would be worth stopping), there are neither enough notable monuments nor notable residents to warrant making a special journey. Yet the newest of all cemeteries, the Gardens of Peace Muslim Cemetery, far out on the eastern reaches of the Central Line at Hainault, is well worth a visit because it is one of only two Muslim cemeteries in London. Its uniform design, which is so different from other cemeteries, has a strange and calming attractiveness.

The main entries inevitably include the 'Magnificent Seven': Abney Park, Brompton, Highgate, Kensal Green, Nunhead, Tower Hamlets, and West Norwood. However, they also take in other notable burial places, some small (for example, Bunhill Fields and Old St Pancras) and some large (for example, St Pancras and Islington), as well as the delightful two burial grounds of St John at Hampstead, and others.

All of these are substantial places, beyond (for many of them) their size. Many have histories that warrant small books: biographies have been devoted to some who are buried in them; architectural enthusiasts visit many just to study their buildings; in some, the flora, fauna and wildlife have caused them to be designated as nature reserves.

However, once the main entries had been decided upon, it seemed wrong not to include others that nevertheless had something to commend them to make them worth a visit even though I did not feel that of themselves they warranted a main entry – it may be who is buried there, a particular style of grave or monument, the history of the place, or even in one case (Greenwich) a magnificent view. They are included in the second section (see And elsewhere…, page 144).

I had not read Simon Jenkins' definition of how he selected England's 1,000 best churches (from about 16,000) in his superb book of the same name when I was making my choices, but I was pleased to find that I had come to the same conclusion: that 'my' burial places, too, had to be 'worth a detour'. Jenkins also said that his churches had to be worth the effort of gaining access. Most cemeteries and burial places can be easily visited – the exceptions are the old and disused Jewish cemeteries, reminders of a rich, immigrant history, which I discuss later in the book – and all I have chosen are freely accessible.

There are some places where the very eminent dead are buried but are not burial places as such. These have not been included for that reason, but the reader can seek out for himself or herself the illustrious interred of Westminster Abbey, the burial place of monarchs and others, St Paul's Cathedral, where Nelson lies, and other places. Brookwood Cemetery is by far the largest of any cemetery at 2,000 acres, but I have also excluded it because it is in Surrey, not London.

So, to decide what to include in either section was, in the end, very much a personal selection informed by places being 'worth a detour'. My choice was also motivated by what I hope will motivate readers: curiosity about the famous and infamous; the unusual and the eccentric; an interest in memorials and architecture, as well as how much we can learn from burial places about people, areas, history and custom; and the sheer delight of walking in what are often such delightful surroundings.

The divisions within Christianity are shown by Catholics having their own cemeteries – the most famous being St Mary's in Kensal Green – and Bunhill Fields being specifically founded for Dissenters, a role then taken on by Abney Park. (The term Dissenters properly refers to any Christian not a member of the Church of England and so includes Catholics, although it tends to be used to describe Nonconformists.) Although the distinction between unconsecrated ground for Dissenters and consecrated ground has mostly disappeared, many public cemeteries still have sections for Catholics. Muslims also often have their own sections, but there are now two Muslim cemeteries in London: the Gardens of Peace Muslim Cemetery in Hainault (included in the main section), and the Waltham Forest Muslim Trust.

Of those Jewish cemeteries open for burial, I chose to include the United Synagogue Cemetery at Willesden. It is generally acknowledged to rank with the other notable London cemeteries, as well as the smaller but interesting

Liberal Synagogue Cemetery which it adjoins. The divisions within Judaism that cause cemeteries to have different affiliations are explained in that entry.

London's Jewish cemeteries are often ancient and recall a community that has sought refuge here at various times – from the Spanish Inquisition to the pogroms of tsarist Russia and on to the Nazi persecution (as well as being expelled from this country at other times). The older cemeteries, often locked, are small and humble places, though they may contain the remains of some of the great and powerful figures of Anglo-Jewry.

London's inner city churchyards are now often public gardens. A few still contain a few tombs and graves, but most commonly, any remains have been removed and the stones placed against surrounding walls. Some churchyards, like their churches, have disappeared entirely: destroyed in the Great Fire of 1666; demolished to make way for housing, road widening or underground stations; or they have simply been demolished for no known reason. Reinterments from many of these churchyards have been carried out in the Victorian cemeteries.

I have not always mentioned war memorials or other public memorials that exist in most large cemeteries, unless there is something unusual or striking about them or about those whom they commemorate. Nor have I made much reference to crematoria nor to those whose ashes are interred.

Some cemeteries continue to be known by their former names (for example, St Marylebone for East Finchley). I have listed both names at the beginning of entries but have otherwise used them interchangeably throughout.

The format, size and style of this book is intended for practical use: as a companion on a visit. The largest cemeteries are often like cities, and, like cities, one can walk set routes or go as the interest takes one. Maps are available for almost all of the places listed and many also offer guide books, both general and specialised, or at the very least leaflets. Noting the paths and who is buried where, I tended to wander around the cemeteries, with the exception of the West Cemetery at Highgate, which can only be visited as part of an organised tour, and Kensal Green, where I chose to join a tour but also made a personal visit. However, in my wanderings, I also made sure that I sought out the most notable graves and monuments. While seeing what there is to see, learning the history and attempting to communicate this to the reader, I have tried, too, to reflect on my own experience as a visitor. I hope that this is evident in the style in which the main entries are written: offering the facts, but also with an impressionistic view, while trying to convey why certain things took my fancy, rather than offering the formal, standard style of many guidebooks.

Details are given about how to reach all places by tube or train. All the burial places are within reasonable walking distance (none more than 20 minutes) of stations. (The one exception is Putney Vale, in the And elsewhere... section where it is necessary to catch a bus after the train journey.)

I have not listed the opening hours as they can change or differ according to the time of year but generally cemeteries are open at 9am and tend to close at 4pm or 5pm. All are open at weekends, except the two Jewish cemeteries at Willesden, both of which close on Saturdays, while the United Synagogue Cemetery is also closed on Fridays.

Guided tours are listed, where available, but not the dates and times, as these can also change from time to time and some are offered according to season. Details can be had by consulting the websites of the Friends' associations or in the case of City of London Cemetery on the website of the City of London Corporation (www.cityoflondon.gov.uk).

The main entries are accompanied (with the exception of where the United and Liberal Jewish cemeteries are to be found) by a recommendation of somewhere to eat and drink. This is often somewhat arbitrary as in some places there is plenty of choice. However, the suggestion is for a drink, a cup of tea and a simple meal, maybe no more than a sandwich or a piece of cake: this is not a guide to the best restaurants.

Information is given for each main entry about something else of interest that readers might want to see while in the area. (The exception here is of Hainault, where the Gardens of Peace Muslim Cemetery is situated, where I could find nothing else to visit.) As with refreshments, this is occasionally an arbitrary selection as one is sometimes spoiled for choice.

Along with the main and secondary entries, there are four other sections. The first is a history of London's burial grounds and cemeteries. Another section describes the meaning of the many symbols to be found atop tombs and graves or cut into headstones. This is far more than decoration: symbolism tells us much about how death, loss and bereavement, religious belief, and personal achievement have been expressed – and, in some respects, still are. Third, I have listed, where possible, interesting or significant people – some well known, some not – interred in each of the main entry cemeteries, but whose names are not included in those entries. Last, there are 10 facts you (probably) did not know about London's cemeteries. There are, of course, many, many more elsewhere in the book.

As I have said, significant interments are the most obvious attraction for visitors, but how the dead are commemorated can tell us a lot, not only about the person, but the societies in which they lived. For example, the pyramids of Egypt were built to prepare the pharaohs for their journey to the afterlife and the Taj Mahal was erected by the Mughal emperor Shah Jahan in memory of his third wife, Mumtaz Mahal. One has to travel abroad to find such flamboyant and magnificent architectural commemorations. Here, our ways are more modest (or not that modest in some cases) but no less informative about the wider society as well as the individual life.

Terry Philpot
Surrey, June 2012

London under ground: a history

In Andrew Miller's award-winning novel, *Pure*, the churchyard of the Church of Holy Innocents in Paris is cleared, the church in the neighbourhood of Les Halles (now site of the Pompidou Centre) is destroyed and the catacombs of Paris are created. The cemetery was shut in 1780, but the danger to public health remains, as the king's minister tells Jean-Baptiste Barratte, the young engineer with whom he charges the tasks of clearance and exhumation and reinterment of remains. The minister goes on to detail other, more fanciful disadvantages, like swoons heard at night, candles pinched by mysterious hands, and moral disturbance among the young. The actual exhumations and removals took place in 1786.

Miller brilliantly weaves a story that was not peculiar to Paris, for the dangers to public health are what led, a few decades after the novel ends, to the creation of the great London cemeteries and the closure of London's churchyards.

Burials were forbidden in city churchyards in London, at Les Innocents and elsewhere in Paris. Montmartre Cemetery was created in the north of the city, Père Lachaise in the east, and Passy in the west, while Montparnasse was created later in the south.

In Britain, it was other cities, not London that led the way in the creation of new large public cemeteries and the move away from crowded and unhygienic city churchyards. Edinburgh's Carlton Hill Cemetery was created in 1792. In 1819, the Rosary Cemetery in Norwich was opened as the first interdenominational cemetery in England. In 1821, Chorlton Row in Manchester followed and four years later came Low Hill in Liverpool. Glasgow's Necropolis was created in 1832, a year before Kensal Green became the first of the new London cemeteries, while in 1834 Key Hill opened in Birmingham, Newcastle General Cemetery in 1835, Sheffield General Cemetery in 1836 and York cemetery in 1836-37.

In the USA, the first out-of-town cemetery to serve a city was Boston's Mount Auburn Cemetery at Cambridge in 1831. Italy, Sweden and France had pioneered landscaped public cemeteries and these examples influenced what was to be created in London. Winding avenues, striking tombs, tree-lined paths, and vistas to suddenly delight the visitor's eye were to be the mark of London's cemeteries, but each very different from the other. However, it was not all borrowing. In 1843, John Loudon propagated ideas about tree planting in his book *On the Laying Out, Planting, and Managing of Cemeteries*. His work influenced not only the new London cemeteries, but also the improvement and design of churchyards.

London, then, was a latecomer to reform and the creation of out-of-town burial places, but the calls that something should be done in the capital reach back long before the Victorian age. Sir Christopher Wren had presciently advocated suburban cemeteries (his proposals were rejected by the City of London) as had his contemporary Sir John Vanburgh on health grounds. In later times and when the problems were becoming acute and physically and olfactorily very obvious, Charles Dickens had complained of 'rot and mildew and dead citizens [that] formed the uppermost scent of the city'. 'Fatal miasmas' were said by others to arise from overcrowded churchyards, where, in some places, corpses were buried only two feet below the surface. There were complaints about 'noxious effluvia', the smell arising from graveyards, and one of the duties of the church sexton was to 'tap' coffins to allow the escape of noxious gases.

Increasing strain had been placed on London's churchyards by the growth of its population. As the city's urban tentacles stretched north, south, east and west, the village churches of Hackney, Lambeth, Stepney and Chelsea were surrounded by new homes. These were built for those streaming in from the country to seek work as agriculture declined and industry prospered, as well as those who came from abroad. As the 19th century progressed, brick and paving spread further in all directions.

Chaucer's London encompassed no further than Temple Bar in the west, Aldgate in the east and Smithfield to the north, with the River Thames providing a natural barrier in the south.

By the reign of George I, London had nearly reached Hyde Park in the west and had gone past the Tower of London in the east, while northwards it was creeping past Holborn and was taking in Southwark south of The Thames. By the end of the 19th century, there were northern suburbs in Hornsey, Tottenham, Hampstead and Walthamstow. Suburbia had marched south as far as Croydon and over to Charlton and Wimbledon, while Richmond, Chiswick and Brentford had succumbed to suburbanisation in the west, and east London now stretched as far as Ilford and Barking.

The city's population was half a million in 1674 and 740,000 by 1760. A hundred years later it had risen to 3,188,485 and in 1913 had topped seven million. In 1842, life expectancy for a professional man was 30 and for a labourer 17. There were 200 graveyards in the capital; high death rates due to infant mortality, epidemics of measles, smallpox, typhoid and cholera were filling them at an alarming rate.

Most churchyards were too small to cope with the numbers of dead. (Peter Ackroyd estimates that Roman London alone was responsible for a million dead.) A small number of gravestones in a churchyard was no sign of the numbers buried there. The churchyard of Christ Church, Spitalfields saw 68,000 people buried there from its opening in 1729 to its closure in 1859. The close packing of the bodies served to preserve them. Soft flesh tissue was still preserved on some of them when they were excavated in 1993. The fact that the churchyard of St Martin-in-the-Fields was only 200 square feet did not prevent it from containing, by the early 1840s, an estimated 60,000 to 70,000 corpses. On 30 September 1838, the *Weekly Despatch*, referring to St Giles' churchyard, said that coffins were buried up to the surface and 'are broken up before they are decayed and bodies are removed to the "bone house" before they are sufficiently decayed to make their removal decent'. St George in the East had three acres for a population of 40,000, while in Bethnal Green, St Matthew's two acres served a population of more than 70,000. The church authorities could only work with what they had: new interments were placed in old graves.

There were exceptions to the general horror. Quaker and Jewish burial places – there are several of the latter in inner London – were uncongested and posed no risk to public health. Even now they are in a good state of repair. Under common law, every parishioner and inhabitant of a parish had a right to be buried in his or her parish churchyard. There were few exceptions to this right of Christian burial, although Nonconformists created their own burial grounds, most famously that of Bunhill Fields. The needs of those who were not members of the Church of England were respected as Victorian public cemeteries were created, and unconsecrated space was set aside for their burial. In one case – Abney Park – a whole cemetery was unconsecrated for just this purpose.

With gross overcrowding, entrepreneurs spotted an opening, and by 1835 there were 14 private, speculatively created burying grounds in existence. One of the attractions for families to inter their dead in such places was that burial fees were cheaper. Some were attached to existing churchyards and burial grounds and some on plots purchased by developers. They were squeezed in on any spare patch of land amid pubs, houses, and work places. There were scandals: undertakers would dress as clergy to perform unauthorised and illegal burials. Bodies were wrapped in cheap material and buried with other dead in graves a few feet deep. Quicklime was often thrown over the body to help speed decomposition to allow a speedy reuse of graves.

Between 1823 and 1848, 5,500 people were interred in one such burying ground in Portugal Street, Holborn. George Alfred Walker, a well-known surgeon and public health reformer, wrote of St James' Burying Ground, Clerkenwell: 'The mortality rate among children in this neighbourhood has been very great. This will not occasion surprise when the locality of the burying ground, and the filth and wretchedness of the major part of the inhabitants, are duly considered ... in the poor ground, little regard is paid to depth of the graves or the removal of the dead. In this filthy neighbourhood, fever prevails and poverty and wretchedness go hand in hand.'

In 1861, in *Night Walk*, Dickens created a picture of London's dead rising to occupy the city: 'It was a solemn consideration what enormous hosts of dead belong to one old great city and how, if they were raised while the living slept, there would not be the space of pinpoint in all the streets and ways for the living to come out into. Not only that, but the vast armies of the dead would overflow beyond the hills and valleys beyond the city, and would stench away all round it, God knows how far.'

Overcrowding, epidemics and risks to health impelled the case for reform, but so did the scandal of these private ventures. The worst of these was the case of the Enon Chapel. This had been built in about 1823 in Clement's Lane (today's St Clement's Lane) in Holborn.

The chapel was divided into two parts by a board floor. Above, religious services were held, below the dead were buried. A corrupt Baptist minister, offering a bargain fee of 15 shillings (75p) for burials, crammed thousands into a pit measuring 12 foot by 59 foot below the chapel. The smell of the rotting dead came up through the floor boards to be breathed in by worshippers, who succumbed to fainting and sickness. When discovered, it was estimated that the unfortunate dead numbered 12,000.

In 1848, the chapel was bought by George Alfred Walker, the surgeon and reformer, who paid for the bodies to be reinterred at West Norwood Cemetery, where they rest in a common grave. Walker disposed of the chapel by lease to George Sanger, a circus impresario, who turned it into a theatre for pantomime and circus. However, he did not stay long, impelled to move by the news that some of the bodies, including that of the minister, were still there. New owners covered the wooden floor beneath which the dead had been crammed, bricked that over, placed a wooden floor on top, and opened what was described as a 'low dancing saloon'. Part of the site is now more dignifiedly occupied by the Royal Courts of Justice.

In 1842, a parliamentary select committee spoke of the need for legislation 'to remedy the evils arising from the interment of bodies within large towns, or of places densely populated'. In that year, too, Edwin Chadwick's *Sanitary Condition of the Labouring Population* found that 20,000 adults and 30,000 children and young people were each year 'imperfectly interred', although it was to be 10 years before legislation barred burials in the inner city.

However, before the creation of the great outer London cemeteries (which preceded the ban on city churchyard burials), there were imaginative schemes that did not see the light of day. Chadwick had hopes of a national cemetery, which, while never realised, perhaps comes nearest with Brookwood, with its 2,000 acres created in Surrey in 1852. Thomas Wilson put forward the idea of a pyramid cemetery at Primrose Hill, north London, for five million Londoners with 40,000 burials a year. This did not come to fruition but Wilson went on to join the board of the General Cemetery Company that created Kensal Green. Another scheme emanated from the mind of Francis Godwin, who suggested a 150-acre neo-classical cemetery, again at Primrose Hill or south of the Thames, near Shooter's Hill. This may seem to presage something of the Magnificent Seven cemeteries and in size rivals cemeteries like the 200-acre City of London, which was opened in 1856.

Practical reform gained real impetus from the grave dangers to public health, sharply focused by the first cholera epidemic in 1832 when more than 6,000 people died in London alone. Between 1831 and 1866 there were four cholera epidemics. Although they were responsible for fewer deaths than other diseases of the time, like influenza and tuberculosis, nevertheless the toll ran in the tens of thousands throughout Britain. The big cities, with their poor and cramped living conditions, were particularly affected.

James Stevens Curl has written that during epidemics, churchyards became 'scenes of the most appalling horror, where bones would be heaped on bones and partially rotting bodies would be disinterred to make way for a multitude of corpses. Coffins would be filled with lime, shrouds dipped in coal tar. Plans to burn bodies immediately after death were defeated by popular uproar'.

The second epidemic in 1848 ushered in, in that same year, the first Public Health Act. Besides other measures, it created a General Board of Health, which could appoint officials and inspectors and create local boards of health. London's board was the Metropolitan Commission of Sewers, and the boards and the commission obtained public health functions with, among other things, responsibility for the burial of the dead.

The Metropolitan Interments Act (1850) gave the Board of Health powers to purchase land on which to open new cemeteries, as well as the power to purchase private cemeteries. This latter power was abolished two years later but not before Brompton Cemetery was taken into public ownership. The board could also advise the Privy Council on the closing of churchyards and other burial places on health grounds and so forbid further burials. This legislation was followed by a succession of the Burial Acts, which were finally rationalised by the Local Government Act (1972). However, importantly, the Burial Act (1852) banned churchyard burials and allowed local vestries to form burial boards to provide burial grounds. (A swift amendment followed to allow cemeteries to be built two miles from the parish boundary.) Hard on its heels, St Pancras Cemetery and St Marylebone Cemetery were both opened in 1854.

Once the need for reform was articulated, its coming was comparatively swift. The transformation from burial in increasingly unsuitable and insanitary churchyards to the creation of large public cemeteries, away from areas of crowded population, was a revolution wrought within a few decades (indeed, Tower Hamlets, the last of the Magnificent Seven, was opened in 1841, more than a decade before the ban on burials in inner city churchyards). Before they were closed for further interments, there were 200 burial places in London – mostly churchyards – but by 1896 more than 90 of them had been dedicated as recreation grounds. Today, only a few inner city churchyards still have more than a nominal number of graves. This movement was assisted, too, by the Disused Burial Grounds Act (1894) (amended by the Open Spaces Act (1887)) and the founding of the Metropolitan Public Gardens Association in 1882.

In May 1830, John Loudon suggested, in the *Morning Advertiser*, that 'there should be several burial grounds, all as far as practicable, equidistant from each other, and from what be considered the centre of the metropolis; that they be regularly laid out and planted with every sort of hardy trees and shrubs; and that in interring, the ground be used on a plan similar to that adopted in the burial grounds of Munich, and not left to chance like Père

Lachaise.' He believed that no expense 'should be spared whatsoever and nurserymen and gardeners be invited to make them botanic gardens'.

Loudon, who is also buried at Kensal Green, which he inspired, is a seminal figure in the reform movement. Born in Scotland, he was a garden designer, cemetery reformer, creator of London's plane trees, a journalist and an encyclopaedist. He contributed to Brompton, Paddington and Westminster cemeteries, and designed Histon Road, Cambridge and Bath Abbey cemeteries. His design for Southampton Old Cemetery was rejected. However he founded one of the first agricultural colleges at Great Tew, while designing Birmingham's Botanical Gardens and the Derby Arboretum.

Reformers like Chadwick and Walker were concerned with public health. Their efforts were complemented by people like George Frederick Carden, a barrister who had visited Paris. There he had been enthused by the design of Père Lachaise as a garden cemetery, with its grand tombs, paths and inclines, and as an alternative to using overcrowded and unhealthy cemeteries in the city. His plan for a 'British Père Lachaise' was turned down in 1824, but undeterred, he put together a committee that became the General Cemetery Company in 1830. It went on to found Kensal Green Cemetery in 1833, the first London commercial cemetery and the first of the Magnificent Seven. Carden is buried there.

It was joint stock (limited liability) companies that created the new cemeteries and they were given powers by Acts of Parliament. Thus, the General Cemetery Company was empowered in 1832 to create a cemetery 'for the interment of the Dead in the neighbourhood of the Metropolis'. Shares at £25 each raised £45,000 to create Kensal Green. Abney Park Cemetery Company also created Chingford Mount, Greenford Park and Hendon Park. In 1836, an Act of Parliament was passed 'for establishing cemeteries for the interment of the Dead, Northward, Southward and Eastward of the Metropolis by a Company to be called The London Cemetery Company'. Stephen Geary, an architect and the company's founder, appointed James Bunstone Bunning as the surveyor and David Ramsey, a renowned garden designer as the landscape architect. A head office was opened at 22 Moorgate Street, London. The company opened Highgate three years later and All Saints at Nunhead in 1840. Both remained in the ownership of these companies and their successors until 1975.

And so, in less than 10 years the Magnificent Seven had come into being: Kensal Green (1833), West Norwood (1836), Highgate (1839), Abney Park (1840), Brompton (1840), Nunhead (1840), and Tower Hamlets (1841).

Catacombs, which Ackroyd calls 'the temples of worship' in the Victorian 'cult of death', were a common feature of the cemeteries. The writer of a guide to Abney Park in 1869 wrote that its catacombs (which can no longer be visited) were 'a cold and stony death place ... the chilliness is awful and repulsive'.

In an enterprise worthy of any undertaken by the Victorians, 305 acres of necropoli were created by a group of architects, landscape designers, sculptors, builders, nurserymen and entrepreneurs in a series of projects that both helped to assist in diminishing a pressing public health problem and created funerary works of art and nature that continue to attract visitors 180 years later. Indeed, one of the most notable aspects of the cemeteries is that they drew together in one place several Victorian fields of achievements – art, architecture, health reform, public institutions and public space.

The new cemeteries were surrounded by high walls, entered through sturdy gates and surveyed from tenanted lodges – such deterrents were believed to be needed to prevent people stealing jewellery from corpses. William Burke and William Hare had been put on trial in 1828. They had murdered 17 people and sold their bodies for dissection. The trial exposed the 'resurrection men', who stole from the graves to meet the needs of anatomy schools. While the Anatomy Act (1832) allowed unclaimed bodies (and the bodies of those whose estates were worth less than a guinea) to be handed over for medical research, it had not wholly deterred what came to be known as 'burkeing' or body snatching for jewellery. (Those with a guinea or more were entitled to a 'guinea funeral' – the simplest of services.)

The pressure for pleasant, spacious cemeteries, situated in rural areas but close to the city and posing no threat to public health, did not cease with the creation of the Seven.

While geography was an important factor in where the dead were buried – east Londoners in Tower Hamlets, those from south London in West Norwood and Nunhead and so on – class, status and wealth had their place among the Victorian dead as much as among the Victorian living. Kensal Green became the fashionable place to be laid to rest, a fact cemented by the burial there of the Duke of Sussex a decade after its gates were opened. St Marylebone catered for the affluent middle classes of Marylebone. Military personnel had special plots set aside in public cemeteries, but they also had had dedicated burial places: soldiers were interred in the Royal Hospital Burial Ground in Chelsea, while the Navy adopted the Royal Hospital Cemetery in Greenwich, although both long preceded the Victorian cemeteries. Between 1855 and 1893, residents of the Royal Hospital, Chelsea were buried in a special plot at Brompton Cemetery and later in Brookwood Cemetery in Woking, Surrey.

There are plenty of public or common (once called pauper) graves to be seen in most cemeteries, although Tower Hamlets is particularly notable in this regard. However, a shared place in an anonymous grave was not the only indignity of many of the poor: they were not even always laid to rest in the areas where they had lived. Brookwood Cemetery was opened as a private cemetery by the London Necropolis and National Mausoleum Company in 1854, and it has been estimated that probably half of east London's dead were buried there under contract from several London boroughs.

The coming of publicly owned cemeteries and the costs of being interred in the Seven and of running them (not to mention the gradual acceptance of cremation) caused their attraction to lessen; most provision now lies with local authorities, who also, in time, took over the management and ownership of some commercial cemeteries. Highgate is owned by the Friends of Highgate Cemetery Trust, and, apart from those cemeteries owned by synagogues, the Catholic Church and the Royal Hospital, Chelsea, eight cemeteries remain in private ownership, including Kensal Green, which is owned by its founders, the General Cemetery Company.

However, neglect, overgrowth and vandalism became the fate of many a great cemetery. Some, like Highgate West, were closed, while with others, like Abney Park, Tower Hamlets and Nunhead, there were plans to clear much of the land. In West Norwood, only legal action stopped the council's destruction of the monuments, many of them listed. These were acts of official vandalism. This sorry state was responsible for the creation of the Friends' associations, which are now so much a part of the continued good fortune of many of the major London cemeteries. They wanted to draw attention to these historically, artistically and sociologically unusual but neglected sites, as well as to ensure that, in some cases, burials could continue. They wanted to ensure that all of them would remain for the interest and delight of future generations.

These were more than places where the dead rested – they could (and did) become how the Victorians had also seen them: places of recreation. Now

Friends' associations engage in preservation and maintenance, create nature trails, draw in school parties, conduct tours and publish guides.

In 1986, the National Federation of Cemetery Friends was created initially by London enthusiasts, but now embraces all associations. Its aim is the conservation of cemeteries, large and small, and to promote understanding and appreciation of them, as well as offering mutual help and support. In 2001, the movement spread abroad when the Association of Significant Cemeteries in Europe came into being.

Much has happened since the earlier pioneers of public health reform set in train what was to become the creation of the great cemeteries – the Magnificent Seven and those that followed quite soon in their wake – that were to ring London.

Extravagant mourning rituals – even the wearing of black at funerals – have largely gone. Clapping has, in some places, replaced silence or a hymn as a coffin is brought up or down the aisle. Pop music is as likely to be played as a hymn or a piece of classical music. Clergy and religious ritual, too, are sometimes now dispensed with in preference for a humanist funeral. Flowers tied to lampposts or on roadsides have become part of the ritual of mourning – often placed by people who have not even known the deceased. The fashion for great tombs, sarcophagi, and mausoleums, which once marked where the honoured dead lie, has all but passed, although in some places quite remarkable memorials have been erected to quite ordinary people – often but not always from Catholic families.

These days nearly three-quarters of the dead disappear into flames rather than the ground, after cremation was ruled legal in 1884. Woodland burials are increasingly popular, albeit by a comparatively small minority.

While some of the older cemeteries still have space, nevertheless it is generally running out in a city where land is tight and the demand for housing and other building is great.

Whatever the vast changes and the challenges, and however different the rising slopes and sepulchral extravagances of, say, Highgate may look from the tamer lawn cemeteries, there is something reassuringly and humanly familiar about a cemetery. No one can be unmoved by the small graves of children, even if they were buried more than a century ago. No one can fail to be inspired by the self-sacrifice – even some small, now forgotten act of heroism – which has brought the person to their rest. The personal tragedies of war, disaster, early death, family misfortune, or the movement of people from one country to another to seek a better life or flee persecution, as many a headstone will testify, resonate through the ages.

Abney Park Cemetery

Stoke Newington High Street N16

Visitors always comment on the extraordinary entrance to Abney Park on Stoke Newington High Street: the Egyptian Revival pylons and railings, with two gatehouses in the style of small temples at either side (the south gatehouse now houses the visitor centre and headquarters of the Abney Park Trust). Indeed, the photograph of the funeral cortege for William Booth, founder of the Salvation Army, in 1912 is as notable for showing the entrance as it is for the crowds who gathered outside.

If you go around the corner and walk along Church Street, which fronts the southern boundary of the cemetery, there is a different, older introduction to Abney Park. A hundred or so yards down Church Street, the magnificent, elegant wrought iron gates were once the entrance to Abney House and led to a winding drive and the elegant house. This was one of two houses that shared the estate on which the cemetery now stands. The other house was Fleetwood House, which was just outside the present walls of the cemetery. The two estates were only combined in 1827, 13 years before the cemetery was founded.

Let us walk back to the main entrance gates. They were built with advice from Joseph Bonomi Junior, the great expert on symbolic decoration and hieroglyphics, who never practised as an architect but was one-time curator of the John Soane Museum in London. Paul Joyce's guide to the cemetery says that Bonomi 'contributed designs for the winged orbs emblematic of eternal life as well as their attendant hieroglyphic legends which translate as "The Gates of the Abode of the Mortal Part of Man"'.

The park was laid out in the 18th century by Lady Mary Abney, although the name Abney was not attached to the mansion until much later. It was called Gunston House, after Thomas Gunston, brother of Lady Mary to whom he had bequeathed his property. For many years, Isaac Watts (1674–1748), the 'father of hymnology', lived here. There is a mound at the upper northwest corner of the cemetery where he is said to have composed some of his hymns, the best known of which is probably 'O God, our help in ages past'. He died here but is, in fact, buried in Bunhill Fields Burial Ground (see page 36). However, his looming statue, on a plinth surrounded by railings, just before the war memorial and in sight of the chapel, looks down the path named after him to the site of where he once lived.

In the early 19th century, the grounds were used, in part, by a Quaker school for girls founded by William Allen and Grizelle Birkbeck. Thus, Abney Park's Nonconformist bona fides were well established when the cemetery was opened by the Lord Mayor of London in 1840. It is the only other major cemetery or burial ground, apart from the no longer used Bunhill Fields, which is unconsecrated. While Catholics and Jews can be considered Dissenters and had no right to be buried in consecrated ground, there is only one headstone with a Hebrew inscription and it is difficult to identify Catholics, if there are any, as religion is not noted in the records.

Abney Park was established as a garden cemetery with an arboretum. It was the first in Europe to be combined with a cemetery.

As Stoke Newington's only nature reserve, there are 200 trees and much flora to be admired. The plan to create a cemetery garden was much assisted by the new owners retaining the lush trees that stood on the old estate. Much of the development we see today, however, has been caused by the woodland seeding itself. The Abney Park Cemetery Trust, which took over the site in 1991, has also begun a helpful practice of placing small, rectangular stones, with an arboreal motif, and the name of the tree in question.

In 2009, more than 170 trees were surveyed and 60 were found to be 'veterans', that is, a tree that is of particular value to wildlife due to damage, decay or old age. Some species can only live in such trees. Two trees, including a holly tree, survive of the 2,500 shrubs and trees originally planted. These included pines, firs and fruit trees, by what was then the nearby Loddiges' nursery, but there are several other trees that are more than 120 years old. Tawny owls, sparrow hawks, wood mice, bats, bank voles and other wildlife find their home here.

At Abney Park's very centre stands the non-denominational Abney Park Gothic chapel, with its turrets and 120 foot spire. Today it is in a sorry state: the windows are open to the elements, one entrance is bricked up, a couple of openings are covered with corrugated iron, and ivy is growing on the outer walls.

Set up by the Abney Park Cemetery Company and the only one of the Magnificent Seven not to be incorporated by individual Act of Parliament, the company sold the cemetery to a commercial company in the 1880s. This kept it going, against several odds, for 100 years until the cemetery was closed in 1978. The company itself went bankrupt in 1974 when the property was placed under legal charge, and was bought by the London Borough of Hackney for a nominal £1 in 1979. In the meantime, as with some other of the great cemeteries, weathering and vandals had done their worst.

The Abney Park Cemetery Trust leased the land as a nature reserve, educational facility, and memorial park. The trust is effectively in charge of the park apart from Hackney's responsibility for the burial functions. The park remains open for the burial of family members of those already interred here, so that one finds a large number of new graves dotted among the older ones and a few interments in existing graves with later names added to headstones.

The park has also been an accredited City and Guilds training centre for over 15 years, has temporary classroom facilities, stone and woodcraft carving workshops, and a children's garden. There are creative and performing arts.

Despite all this activity, the overwhelming impression is that here is one of the country's great cemeteries, ranking with any of the other Seven. It may not have such a publicly distinguished population as Highgate, Kensal Green or Brompton. It does not have so unusual and attractive an addition as the Greek necropolis at West Norwood, but it has all the romantic eeriness that one finds at Nunhead – appropriately enough as the American Gothic novelist Edgar Allen Poe attended a school nearby around 1820.

The poet Robert Southey is said to have called Abney Park the Dissenters' 'Campo Santo'. In fact, as he died in 1843, three years after it opened, he more likely gave that title to Bunhill Fields (see page 36) but Abney Park's enthusiasts seem to have taken it for their own; understandably so, as it has long far outranked Bunhill Fields both in size and the variety of Nonconformists and others buried here. Numerous clergymen are interred here, including John Harris DD (1802–1856), principle of New College, London, and the grey obelisk of the Rev Edward Mannering (1801–1875) testifies to his 50 years as minister of the various chapels at Jewry Street, Holywell Mount and Bishopsgate.

A notable political dissenter buried here is Samuel Morley (1809–1885), the MP for Nottingham and later Bristol, and an abolitionist, who lived on Stamford Hill, which is no distance from the main entrance gates. His large but simple tomb, with a plain pediment, is on Dr Watts' Walk. Another politician is Henry Richard (1812–1888), who combined that calling with being a Congregational minister. His impressive Gothic shrine has a sculpted bas-relief portrait. The Chartist (James) Bronterre O'Brien (1805–1864), the most famous of these political activists, rests here.

The high-minded are not only to be found in this soil, however. Albert Chevalier (1861–1923), music hall star who popularised the song 'My

Old Dutch', lies here, too. Or, to give him his full name, Albert Onesime Britannicus Gwathveoyd Louis Chevalier, evidence of his French-Welsh parentage. He lies with his father-in-law, also a noted music hall performer, Joe Sanders (1842–1884), better known as George Leybourne or 'Champagne Charlie'. Leybourne died penniless in Islington. His headstone tells us that 'God's finger touched him and he slept'. Florence Isabella Chevalier (died aged 63), who may have been Chevalier's sister, is also buried here with Chevalier's son, Frederick George (died aged 22).

The original catchment area for the cemetery stretched as far as the City of London, as some addresses on the memorials testify. The cemetery also speaks of a more middle class area than Stoke Newington has since become, despite more recent gentrification: GPs, JPs, professional people, businessmen, local councillors, and army officers lie side by side. Among them, a white marble baroque angel stands on a polished granite pedestal to look down on Sir William Johnson (1845–1912), an original member of the London County Council and a Lord Mayor of London. Yet, at its foundation, the cemetery was to be very specifically, said the owners, 'open to all classes of the community' and its comparatively low fees made it attractive for that reason.

The main paths curve northwards from the main entrance and cross at various points. A few of these are lined with small headstones, which, at one time, marked common graves. They were moved when paths were dug up and then restated for common grave burials. Also running from these paths are smaller ones, which are not always easy to walk down, that lead deeper into undergrowth. They offer glimpses of fallen or broken memorials, headstones askew, and some are sunken into the ground or covered in ivy or brambles. (There are, though, plenty of memorials and stones to see in a similar state just by sticking to the main paths).

It is difficult, when walking around, to agree with the cultural historian Ian Sinclair when he writes that the 'wilderness of oak and chestnut, swamp cypress, thistle, Japanese knotweed, has been fiercely hacked by community miscreants'. By this, one assumed, in 1997, he meant the Trust. And he goes on: 'Abney Park has been demystified. It has lost its patina of obscurity'. Given the present state, demystification is hard to appreciate, so one can only imagine what matters were like then.

Given the plainness and modesty of nonconformity, there is an impressive collection of memorials, not as striking or as monumental as, say, Highgate,

but well worth the effort to seek out. An effigy of a life-sized sleeping lion, in white marble, seemingly stands guard, on the tomb of Frank Bostock (1866–1912), his wife Catherine (1865–1929), their four adult children, and 'our darling little "Sophie"', Emma Sophie Susie, who died in June 1886 aged four months and two weeks. Other relatives (and a family friend) lie in the same tomb.

John Jay (1805–1872), a stone mason and builder, rests on Dr Watts' Walk, in a Grade II listed, baroque style, white marble sarcophagus with a moulded cover and lions' feet at the corners. It is said that this was constructed in his own workshop and possibly by the man himself. It would be an excusable self-aggrandisement, for he not only created the entrance to the cemetery and the chapel, but was also responsible for several outstanding buildings, including Colchester, Paddington and other railway stations, the Royal Earlswood Hospital, Surrey, and Billingsgate market.

The grave of William Booth (1829–1912), founder of the Salvation Army, his wife Catherine (1829–1890) and those of their relatives lie a short distance to the left of the main entrance on Abney House Corner, with their headstone in the shape of an Army shield of blue Pennant sandstone and gilt inscriptions. Opposite, there are other Salvationists' graves in the same style, including that of the Booths' son, William Bramwell Booth (1856–1929), the Army's first chief of staff who succeeded his father as general.

Just along on the same path, a modern memorial catches the eye. This is the rectangular, black marble stone of Salvation Army Commissioner Robert Hoggard (1861–1935). It is divided in two, with an inscription in English on one side and in Korean on the other. It was put up in 2008. It recounts his going to evangelise in Korea, on instruction from William Booth. He was territorial commander there from 1908 to 1918 and went by the Korean name of Huh Gab-doo.

A small but striking and exceptionally well-maintained memorial on Path T is the grave of William Frederick Tyler, a police constable who, at the age of 31 on 23 January 1909, was killed in Tottenham 'bravely doing his duty'. He was shot in the head by gunmen when pursuing them after a robbery by anarchists in the famous Tottenham Outrage (a 12-year-old boy was also murdered), two years before the Siege of Sydney Street (see City of London Cemetery, page 42). Tyler's memorial has a red marble base with a white marble canopy, in the baroque style, below which is a white marble policeman's helmet and folded cape. It is topped by a cross with his number, 403, engraved below.

The large war memorial by the chapel, with steps that approach the traditional Blomfield 'Cross of Sacrifice' and names engraved on metal plaques, has been so well refurbished that it now belies its age (it was first erected for the dead of the First World War). The cemetery's only catacomb is, in fact, under the war memorial. Some years ago, the entrance to the catacomb was filled in because skeletons were removed by intruders interested in black magic.

There are several military headstones nearby and others are elsewhere in the cemetery. In a less happy state than that of the war memorial is the memorial to civilian dead, found just before the Watts' statue. Some of the commemorative lettering has disappeared. There are nearly 150 names of people who died in seven streets between 1940 and 1944, most from the Coronation Avenue incident, when nearly everyone was killed in an air raid shelter that suffered a direct hit in 1940.

At least two people took pride in stating their long association with where they had lived: William Stiles (died aged 68 in 1868), 'an old inhabitant of

Shoreditch', who has a flat-topped red granite column. While near the old Bhutan Pine, on Road 1, the grave of Samuel Bateman can be found (died aged 76 in 1845), 'a very old inhabitant of St Leonard's, Shoreditch', along with his wife Sarah, who outlasted him by 23 years and died aged 83.

Walter Vooght (died aged 81 in 1938), erected a large black marble memorial, on top of which is a large cross, to his wife, Harriet (who predeceased him by four years at the age of 67). He rests with her. On the pavement base is a statue of a woman holding a wreath. Unfortunately, she has lost her head. Another female figure – this time with all parts attached – can be found on Road C. She is bowed in deep mourning or prayer, her elbows resting on a short column placed on a massive raised pedestal. This is the grave of Fanny Mechi (1799–1845), first wife of John Joseph Mechi, a Stamford Hill resident whose hopes of becoming Lord Mayor of London were dashed by his financial problems and eventual bankruptcy.

The cemetery may long ago have replaced the bucolic charms of the estate, with its handsome houses, on which it was built. However, it has its own charms and great interest; its revival as a nature reserve has restored it to the verdant state that the cemetery's first owners foresaw for it, after so many years of changing fortunes and downright neglect.

Getting there
Stoke Newington Rail Station

Friends' association
Yes

Tours
Yes

Take a break
Circo, 170 Stoke Newington High Street N16

Something else to see
St Matthias Church, Wordsworth Road N16

Brompton
Cemetery

Fulham Road SW10

In an age of cemetery creation when restraint was no impediment to the creators, Brompton Cemetery overstretched itself and nearly succumbed to over-ambition.

Lord Kensington sold what was a market garden in the then open countryside of west London to the West London and Westminster Cemetery Company (a picture from 1865 shows the cemetery still surrounded by fields). The company appointed the inventor and entrepreneur Stephen Geary, best known for his work as an architect at Highgate Cemetery (see page 74), as architect, but a competition awarded the job to Benjamin Baud, an architect, who had worked on the rebuilding of Windsor Castle. Geary had been eligible to enter the competition, but he was asked to resign. He sued the company and lost. And thus, on an unpromising site – a half mile long, flat, treeless rectangle – Baud created the new cemetery. It opened in 1840 and then became known as the West of London and Westminster Cemetery. In 1844, another 4.5 acres were added at what is now the Fulham Road end, with a purchase from the Equitable Gas Company.

Baud was constrained neither by the unpropitious nature of the land nor by any limit to his grandiose visions. Although when defects were later found in the buildings, he was sacked, sued for money owed, lost and gave up architecture. However, what we see today is very much his vision. He envisaged an immense open air 'cathedral' and saw that the rectangle lent itself to precisely that. His 'nave' (the Central Avenue) is almost the length of the cemetery. It is flanked by two colonnades and runs a third of the way down the site to the 'high altar' (the domed Anglican chapel). It is interrupted by the 300 foot Great Circle, said to be inspired by the piazza of St Peter's in Rome, beneath which the catacombs are reached by several broad steps (guided tour only). Baud created a symmetrical design with two 'aisles' (main paths) running parallel to each side of the 'nave'.

Two additional chapels, for Catholics and Dissenters, were seen by Baud as forming 'transepts' on either side of the Great Circle. Baud's 'great west door' was the magnificent triumphal arch he designed for the main Old Brompton Road entrance. (The park keepers' office is at this end. The South Lodge at the Fulham Road entrance, which is a five minute walk from Fulham Broadway tube station, is home to the Friends' association and has maps and publications.)

During spring and summer, this place is a riot of colour and foliage. Fifty distinctive types of tree have been identified and there are bluebells

(February), daffodils (March), cow parsley (May), sweet pea (July) and other flowers, spread among the graves and lining the paths. Looking down the Central Avenue, lined by lime trees with rows of taller pines outside of these, toward the Old Brompton Road entrance, there are the colonnades on either side fronted by graves and the cemetery seems to spread to where the colonnades end. This is a sight to gladden the eye. Viewed from the Old Brompton Road entrance, the colonnades could easily be taken to be the kind of architectural feature that one finds in some of the great cemeteries on the French battlefields of the First World War. Brompton is not on the English Heritage Register of Parks and Gardens and a conservation area for no reason.

What we see now came about despite the shareholders of the company initially balking at Baud's ambitious schemes, for he was allowed to proceed at increased expense. One result of some need to rein in costs was that the two other chapels were never built. (It is said that anti-Catholic feeling caused the Catholic chapel not to see the light of day, which led to the creation in 1858 of St Mary's Catholic Cemetery, Kensal Green (see page 116) with some exhumations taking place at Brompton for reinterment there.)

Baud may have seen most of his 'cathedral' arise among the bucolic charms of west London, but the shareholders gained little return for their money and he was sacked in 1840. In the wake of concerns about the operations of private investors in cemeteries, the Metropolitan Interments Act (1850) was passed to allow the Board of Health to provide publicly owned cemeteries. Although repealed two years later, this act of necropolitan socialism let shareholders salvage something when the sale went through in 1852 for £74,921.14s. The owners, the West of London and Westminster Cemetery Company, had wanted £166,762.12s 8d. However, 1852 was also the year that the legislation was repealed and Brompton remains the only cemetery ever to have been nationalised. It is now owned by the Department of Culture, Media and Sport and for the last 50 years has been managed by the Royal Parks.

It is probably this management that has ensured that this is a well-tended place – there is none of the managed neglect one finds in Highgate or of the ivy-clad, half hidden memorials of Nunhead. Closed for burials at one time, Brompton was reopened and among more recent interments, the flat headstones of the writer and critic Bernard Levin (1928–2004) and 'wrestler, actor, writer' Brian Glover (1934–1997) can be found among the older graves.

This good management means that it is a very easy cemetery to walk around, and one can easily step between the graves and tombs. Almost all graves are

visible, and none are more than a few feet from a path, from which they can mostly be seen.

Squirrels are constant companions for visitors. The slight disadvantage of Brompton is that it is a useful cut-through from Old Brompton Road to Fulham Palace Road, which means that most people one sees – including the ubiquitous cyclists – are too busy getting elsewhere (or speaking loudly on

their mobile phones) to stop, admire and contemplate the natural and man-made wonders about them.

One unusual design aspect of Brompton is the circles created by tapering the ends of paths. These circles were meant to be sold to allow the wealthy to build their mausoleums there, but this was realised in only one case: that of Hannah Courtnoy whose massive, 40-foot high, polished Egyptian-style mausoleum dominates the upper eastern side of the grounds. It is an unusual (maybe unique) structure, for it bears no inscription. The Royal Parks official guide says that little is known about her other than that she died in 1854, was unmarried and is buried here with two of her daughters (a third daughter and son-in-law are buried on the East Terrace). However, a couple of genealogy websites give her date of death as 1849 (she died aged 62 as reported in *The Times*) and her family surname as Peters. It is rumoured that she may have been a royal mistress.

Near Courtnoy's spot is the tiered memorial that Alfred Mellon (1820–1867), violinist and leader of the Covent Garden Ballet Orchestra, had erected for his wife, the Shakespearean actress, Sarah Jane Woolgar (1824–1909). This may seem curious in that he predeceased her but, at that time it was not uncommon for memorials, especially striking ones like this, to be erected while the intended inhabitant was alive. One assumes that that is what happened here. In further deference to what one assumes were his feelings for her, he had himself buried under a simple stone nearby, although both (unusually for Brompton) are so covered in ivy that the inscription cannot be seen.

There are a very large number of military burials at Brompton boosted by the fact that between 1855 and 1893, 2,625 Chelsea Pensioners were interred here, in their own section, when interments ceased at the Royal Hospital cemetery (see And elsewhere... page 144). There are 12 VCs, including two from the Crimea. The white memorials of the Coldstream Guards stand to dignified attention behind railings. There are also several military headstones scattered about nearby and not only for the British fallen – among them are numbered South Africans and Czechs.

James MacDonald (1843–1915), a Scotsman who helped found Standard Oil, gave himself a flamboyant Gothic mausoleum that stands close to several Polish graves. At one time, this was the most popular last resting place for members of the Polish community in exile (many of whom settled in west London, where many Poles still live today). The site is said to contain: one admiral; one wing commander; 12 generals; 47 colonels; two prime ministers, Tomasz Arciszewski (1877–1952) and Lt General Stawoja Sktadkowski (1885–1962); the bishop of the Polish Orthodox Community and chaplain to the 2nd Corps, Archbishop Sawa (1898–1951); and 275 others. Despite the eminence of some of these, all the graves and stones are simple and are placed over a large area stretching out from behind the MacDonald mausoleum.

Also here is the simple grave of Dr John Snow (died 1858), who discovered the link between contaminated water and cholera, a disease that had done so much to fill London's churchyards. He was also a pioneer of anaesthesia and administered chloroform to Queen Victoria during childbirth. Frances (Fanny) Brawne (1800–1865), the fiancée of John Keats, can also be found beneath a simple stone.

By flamboyant contrast, there are the copper-roofed and bronze arabesques on the marble tomb of Frederick Leyland (died 1892), ship owner and

patron of artists. This is the only tomb ever designed by the Pre-Raphaelite Edward Burne-Jones.

It is the nature of cemeteries that there are unlikely bedfellows close to one another; here Emmeline Pankhurst (1858–1928), suffragette leader and founder of the militant Women's Social and Political Union, rests beneath a Celtic cross of Northamptonshire Marlstone with a bas-relief Christ offering a blessing in the style of Eric Gill on its stem. Only a few places away is the resting place of Richard Tauber (1891–1948), the renowned Austrian-born tenor and exponent of Mozart. (The conductor Sir Thomas Beecham chose him for the first full-length recording of *The Magic Flute*). His is a large, simple, dark grey slab of a headstone with a cross (adorned with flowers the day I was here) and has below it a small, black marble stone with a quotation from the writer AP Herbert, paying tribute to 'that rich, rolling, tender' voice.

Brompton commemorates three especially interesting minor characters, one of whom is now absent. Chief Long Wolf (1833–1892), who led his tribe in the Sioux Wars only to die in England when performing with Buffalo Bill's Wild West Show, is no longer here. In 1997, his remains were removed to the Wolf Creek Community Cemetery, South Dakota. Today, the site of his former grave is marked by a large cross, engraved with a running wolf. His fellow American, Colonel Henry Byrne (1838–1915), is buried with his wife and daughter in a handsome, red marble tomb. He fought as a mercenary for Garibaldi in the campaign for Italian unification, for the North in the American Civil War, and for the British in South Africa. The attractions of a quieter life led him (one imagines) to become mayor of New Romney in Kent and a justice of the peace. Proudly but perhaps forgivably, copies of his medals are carved on the tomb.

Last of this remarkable trio is George Henry Borrow (1803–1881), a now forgotten novelist who extolled the gypsy life of the outdoors, beer drinking and bare knuckle fighting. By the time he was 16, he was said to speak seven languages and was reputed later to have mastered 35, as well as translating part of the New Testament into Catalan. Until 1939, gypsies gathered annually at a festival in the cemetery to commemorate their champion.

Among all the inscriptions extolling the virtues of the dead, their loss to the world, their roles as loving mothers and fathers, staunch patriots and notable public figures, one deserves special mention: opposite the guards' burial plot is a headstone to Gavin Hodge (1944–2009) and his 10-year-old daughter. He was, we are told, a 'hairdresser, hedonist, father and friend'. What story lies beneath that grey granite stone?

There is an immortality of a sort here, different from that symbolised by the grand memorials and eloquent inscriptions: think of Beatrix Potter, who lived in nearby Kensington as a child. She is not buried here (she was cremated and her ashes scattered in Cumbria), but, as a child, she would have run among the graves, laughing at some of the names inscribed on the memorials, but also lodging them in her mind. Later in life, she gave a kind of immortality to some of those whom she remembered and denied those whose names were far better known in their lifetimes: Peter Rabbett and a Jeremiah Fisher are to be found here, along with a Brock, and a Nutkins.

Getting there
Fulham Broadway or West Brompton tube stations

Friends' association
Yes

Tours
Yes

Take a break
The Troubadour, 263–267 Old Brompton Road SW5

Something else to see
Brompton Oratory, Brompton Road SW3

NEAR BY LIE THE REMAINS OF
THE POET-PAINTER
WILLIAM BLAKE
1757 — 1827
AND OF HIS WIFE
CATHERINE SOPHIA
1762 — 1831

Bunhill Fields Burial Ground

City Road EC1

Bunhill Fields, the world's foremost Dissenters' burial ground, is now one of the few reminders of the City before the Great Fire of London. It sits, appropriately enough, between two other reminders of the British Nonconformist tradition.

Wesley's Chapel stands across from the gate in City Road (and where, incidentally, a Denis Thatcher took a Margaret Roberts as his second wife). A statue of Charles Wesley, that church's founder and most famous preacher, guards the chapel's courtyard and looks down on the part-marble obelisk to his mother Susanna (1669–1742), whose grave is across the road. Her son is actually buried in the graveyard behind his chapel.

On the other side of Bunhill Row at the eastern side of the Fields is an important but far less imposing place: Quaker Gardens. This was formerly the Quaker Burial Ground, now it is a rather sad, neglected and scrawny spot – a small public garden, partly a children's playground, overlooked by a tower block. There is no indication now (except for a small sign) of its former existence, as Quakers did not have tombstones, so the Society's founder George Fox (1624–1691) rests somewhere below the patchy grass and concrete along with 12,000 others of his creed. Wartime bombing and post-war redevelopment did for the Society's 'coffee tavern', a medical mission, and meeting house (built in 1861) that once stood here. The surviving former caretaker's house is now the meeting house.

In fact, this is the original Bunhill Fields, for while the present renowned burial ground was opened in about 1665 as a place for Dissenters to be laid to rest, the Quakers were here first: the first Bunhill Fields, which was also the first Quaker-held freehold in the capital, was opened for all London Quaker burials in 1661. There is no record of Bunhill Fields being consecrated and Nonconformists were buried here because they could only be buried elsewhere with the use of *The Book of Common Prayer.*

The derivation of the name from 'Bone Hill', a burial site, may show an even longer funerary history: this has been a place for the dead to rest for more than 1,000 years. (The name may, alternatively, refer to the practice, a century or so before Bunhill Fields's foundation, of bringing the bones from the charnel house of St Paul's Cathedral to make way for new burials. The bones were dumped and lightly covered by earth.)

Reached by way of Moorgate tube, with its several exits, one arrives at Bunhill Fields through the maze of glass and metal towering buildings that has come to characterise this ancient edge of London's financial district. (Old Street tube station is a five-minute, uncomplicated walk away.) One side of Bunhill Fields runs along the busy City Road that the nursery rhyme tells one to go 'up and down', while The Eagle public house, in which to go in and pop one's weasel, is still in nearby Shepherdess Walk.

The burial ground is Grade I listed for its historic landscape. It is also within the Bunhill Fields and Finsbury Square Conservation Area and has 75 listed tombs. The present state derives from two significant phases: the improvement by the City of London in 1860, which included the avenues of plane trees (after its closure for burials it reverted to an 'Open Space' to the City of London Corporation for its upkeep by an Act of Parliament in 1867) and the 1960s' conversion to a 'garden of rest'. This 'tidying up' gives the place a far more ordered and formal look than it would have had originally; certainly, it is far more formal than the great Victorian cemeteries that came 200 years after its creation.

However, it might not have been like that. The legislation of 1867 only came about because that year, the estate, attached to St Paul's who owned it, passed to the Ecclesiastical Commissioners. Their plans to make use of the land for development were stopped only when Parliament stepped in and turned the site over to the City of London and, after restoration, it was opened to the public in 1869.

The burial ground was severely damaged by enemy bombing in the Second World War, hastening the creation in 1960 of the public park. The public gardens of today account for half of what was the burial site.

The burial ground is recognised as a Site of Importance for Nature Conservation. As well as planes, other trees include the Norway maple, sycamore, chestnut, lime, oak, ash, fig and mulberry. Birds spotted here include the great tit, blue tit, wren and robin. The spotted flycatcher, a priority species of the UK Biodiversity Action Plan, is reported to be breeding on the site. In the spring, the graves are carpeted by snowdrops, daffodils and hyacinths.

Visitors seeking other forms of relaxation in the summer months can enjoy Tai Chi, 'free bike surgery', yoga, reiki, massage, a history tour and talks on urban wildlife by the National History Museum.

The burial ground is easy to view: it is comparatively small – although by the time it closed for burials in 1854, about 123,000 people were buried here

(even though Elizabeth Oliver, aged 15, is said to have managed to get herself buried here in 1884 by means of a vault being reopened) and there are more than 2,500 memorials. A main path, with graves either side, runs from one entrance to the other, with paths off that. Most graves are within railings, however one railinged area has no path and seems to have no means of entry. The railing gates are locked and one is asked to only enter with an attendant, but, alas, the attendant's cabin has limited opening hours that are not listed (or not very obviously). However, there are many graves that are not within the railings and many of those can be seen from the paths.

Fortunately, the three monuments that most people want especially to see are not within the railings, are close to one another and are near the attendant's office. These are the grave of the poet and mystic William Blake (1757–1827); the memorial to the novelist Daniel Defoe (1661–1731); and tomb of the great Nonconformist itinerant preacher and writer, John Bunyan (1628–1688).

Defoe's burial here is all the more appropriate as he referred to this place in his *A Journal of the Plague Year* (1722), when he wrote of 'many [plague victims], who were infected and near their end, and delirious also, ran wrapped in blankets and rags and threw themselves in [the mass burial plague pits] and expired there'.

Blake and Defoe (he was born Foe but his memorial calls him De-foe) are commemorated next to one another, though neither monument is quite as they seem. The tombstone of Blake ('the poet-painter') says that he and his wife,

Catherine Sophia (1762–1831), are buried 'nearby' and Defoe's handsome tombstone, once lost, now sits in the Hackney Museum, three miles away (he was educated and lived in Stoke Newington). His obelisk was raised in 1870 after (as it says) an appeal for funds to the boys and girls who read *The Christian World*. It was restored in 1948 and does not look like it has been touched since. The inscription does say that it was raised 'upon his grave', so we can assume that the author of *Robinson Crusoe* lies beneath it, whereas Mr and Mrs Blake are not below the paving stones on which their headstone is placed.

Bunyan's resting place, where this pilgrim's progress ended (at least in the worldly sense), is impressive, despite being very weather worn and covered in lichen. It is a large table tomb, surrounded by railings, with his recumbent effigy, added in 1862, on top.

Among other notable graves is the well-preserved one for Susanna (1669–1742). She was not only mother of Charles and John Wesley but also 17 others, something she must have taken in her stride, as she was the 25th of her parents' 25 children. John himself conducted her funeral in front of large crowds. She is along the path from Henry Cromwell, grandson of Oliver. Or possibly not because rather confusingly, the City of London's otherwise useful information leaflet says that Henry is buried here with 'many other Cromwell relatives' (in fact, there are believed to be 13). The notice on the attendant's cabin says that Henry bought two graves, in memory of his family, but adds that he is buried in Lisbon where he died in 1711. (One Cromwell who is not here is the unfortunate Oliver, who in 1661, after the Restoration, was exhumed from his vault in Westminster Abbey, posthumously executed, his body hanged in chains at Tyburn, and then thrown into a pit. His head changed hands several times and is now believed to be buried in the grounds of Sydney Sussex College, Cambridge.)

One Cromwell relative who is here is the Lord Protector's son-in-law, General Charles Fleetwood (c1618–1692). There are other errors about burials here, too: John Hone Tooke is said to rest here when he is buried in Ealing churchyard.

The hymnologist Isaac Watts (1674–1748) is also buried here, but he is more strikingly commemorated by a statute on a tall column at Abney Park (see page 18). 'Satan finds some mischief still, for idle hands to do', he wrote in his poem, *Against Idleness and Mischief*. These were never faults to which he fell prey: he wrote 750 hymns.

One of the most intriguing tombs is that of Dame Mary Page, wife of the wealthy London merchant Gregory Page, who was a shipwright and director of the British East India Company. She died at the age of 56 in 1728. The inscription on a panel of her cracked and severely weathered tomb tells us that 'In 67 months she was tapped 66 times ... 240 gallons of water drawn without ever repining at her case or ever fearing the operation'. It has been suggested that having such drastic excessive fluid drained may have been to treat Meig's Syndrome.

Across the path there is also a headstone for Rev Alexander Waugh (1754–1827), one of the founders of the London Missionary Society (and ancestor of the novelist, Evelyn Waugh), his wife, children and sister-in-law, and another clergyman and his wife. This replaced a former memorial. A colleague of Waugh's lies nearby in a family grave: Joseph Hardcastle (1752–1819). As 'a merchant of the City of London', he was not only founder of the British and Foreign Bible Society, but also an associate of William Wilberforce in the campaign to abolish slavery.

Bunhill Fields has tended to be overshadowed, in size and the numbers buried there, by its successor, Abney Park (see page 18). However, this takes nothing from the interest and beauty of this hallowed, unique little spot in the city.

Getting there
Old Street tube station

Friends' association
No

Tours
Yes

Take a break
The Artillery Arms, Bunhill Row EC1

Something else to see
Wesley's Chapel and House, City Road EC1

City of London Cemetery

Aldersbrook Road E12

LEFT:
Anglican Chapel

to mass reinterments that are not from churchyards. This is the large upright granite rock for French Protestants and their descendants, who were in the Charitable Hospital for Poor French Protestants, Finsbury. This would have been more like a workhouse, which served the poor of this community in Bath Street. Also to be seen is the Gothic screen for those who were in the Royal Infant Orphanage in nearby Wanstead. Other memorials commemorate those reinterred from the burial ground of Newgate Prison, on the site of where the Old Bailey now stands, and Christ's Hospital.

There is also an interesting tall black marble Art Deco headstone here, with its gold motif for Frederick Herbert Light (died aged 58 in 1935) and other family members. Sadly, the surround for the checkerboard-patterned base is broken.

Dame Anna Neagle (1904–1986), the actress and her film director and producer husband Sir Herbert Wilcox (1892–1977) would have been known by many of those lesser folk among whom they now rest. Interestingly, both are buried in a Neagle family grave, with their names at the very bottom. She is referred to by her married name as Florence Marjorie Wilcox DBE. His CBE is listed but not his knighthood.

The cemetery has a good number of mausoleums and while that of the Pedley family (where Anchor Road meets Belfry Road) may not be the most attractive, few others anywhere can hold no less than 28 family members.

A memorial of a different kind is that of Gladys Spencer (1897–1931), a popular teacher and trainer of child dancers and performers at the local Classical Academy of Music and Dance. Her local fame, allied with the tragedy of her early death from pneumonia, has created a memorial that shows a reclining, sad-eyed woman resting on the keyboard of a grand piano – an exact copy of that bought for her by her brothers. Her father was a market gardener and the inscription reads, in part: 'The gardener hath plucked a still rarer flower'.

However, this cannot compare with the commemoration of David John Vigiland. He would not be remembered now had he remained buried in Mombasa, Kenya, where, a member of the Royal Navy, he died aged 20 in 1946. He was his parents' only son and they had his body brought home for reburial here on 9 December 1952 on what would have been his 26th birthday. Above him they erected the most remarkable of memorials to be seen anywhere. Carved in Italy from a 25-tonne block of Sicilian marble, it has a large base that supports a podium, above which is a life-size representation of Christ being taken from the cross by seven other figures.

What the City of London lacks in great memorials or a large number of the illustrious dead, it more than makes up for not only in the quiet beauty of its surroundings, but the interesting and unique lights it shines on the history of the areas from which many of those buried here came.

Getting there
Manor Park and Woodgrange Park rail stations

Friends' association
Yes

Tours
Yes

Take a break
Aldersbrook Conservation Area E12

Something else to see
Wesley's Chapel and House, City Road EC1

East Finchley (St Marylebone) Cemetery

East End Road N2

East Finchley Cemetery announces its attractions immediately. The black railings lead the visitor to the arched stone entrance and just inside there is an impressive Gothic lodge and two spreading cedar trees. There is no long avenue to walk or vast courtyard to cross to find what the place holds, for immediately in view are two of the cemetery's most striking attractions.

The first and most obvious is the ragstone Anglican Church in the Gothic style. This is actually called a 'church' rather than a 'chapel' – there is a plainer, more attractive Dissenter's chapel, also in the Gothic style, dating from 1854, a short distance away. The church's size is deceptive: it can hold 100 people. It has an exit (now blocked) that slyly allowed coffins to be taken directly into the cemetery, as opposed to back up the aisle, out and then back round the building.

The second sight that catches the eye on entry is to the left of the church: the imposing red granite memorial to Sir Peter Nicol Russell (1816–1865). He was an engineer, born in Kirkcaldy, Scotland and died in London, who founded the Peter Nicol Russell School of Engineering at the University of Sydney, New South Wales. A copy of the monument stands outside the school.

A fine bust of Sir Peter surmounts his tall column and below stands a life-sized, bare-chested workman, wrought in bronze. He has a hammer in his hand and anvil and cogwheel at his feet, while slightly above him hovers an angel, one hand on the workman's shoulder. The name of Sir Peter's widow, Dame Charlotte, who died in 1911, is inscribed below, but I have been unable to discover what earned her the damehood.

However, Dame Fanny Houston (1857–1936) was one of the first dame commanders of the British Empire and gained her honour for founding the Rest Home for Retired Nurses in the First World War. She was also a suffragist, philanthropist and a famous eccentric. She inherited £5.5 million from her third husband, branded Ramsay MacDonald's National government 'unpatriotic', and had previously opposed his Labour government when it refused her offer of £200,000 to strengthen the Navy and Army. She died of a heart attack when she stopped eating after having been upset at the abdication of Edward VIII. Her grave, marked by a headstone, is on Remembrance Avenue.

The perfectly kept acres and clearly signposted roads on its 47 acres make East Finchley Cemetery almost an intimate place – perhaps especially so for a municipal cemetery, which are often very large, like the nearby Finchley Cemetery (see page 56). This one is very easy and pleasant to navigate. It is

largely formal parkland, with flower beds and mature trees lining the avenues. There is no undergrowth and graves are well spaced. All tombstones can be viewed, comparatively few are broken or fallen, none appear to be buried, and all the inscriptions I saw were decipherable. Indeed, every grave I was seeking I found simply by walking around, unaided by a map.

Walking southwards, the land falls away gently, giving an impression of great calm. The 1960s' extension is unexceptional but even its visual disadvantages have been offset by judicious planting. It is not surprising that Keep Britain Tidy awarded the cemetery its Green Flag accreditation for the best green open space in the years 2007 to 2011.

There are a couple of metal maps that show the cemetery's layout but point only to one monument – its central glory – the Glenesk mausoleum. This was built for Algernon Borthwick (1830–1908), the first Lord Glenesk, one time Conservative MP and owner of *The Morning Post*, which merged with *The Daily Telegraph* in 1937; appropriate, then, for a cemetery intended for the affluent middle classes of north London. His wife and son also rest here. They predeceased him and when he died the title became extinct. The mausoleum stands at the very centre of the cemetery in the middle of a circle, where avenues meet. It was encircled by builders' fencing when I visited it as it is unsafe. It is on the grand scale as mausoleums go: a small Gothic chapel in the Decorated style. Inside there are three alabaster sarcophagi before a marble reredos and stained glass windows. Designed by Sir Arthur Blomfield, architect of the Law Courts and the Royal College of Music among other buildings, it is Grade II listed.

To the left of the mausoleum is the red granite memorial, with bas-relief, to Sir Henry Rowley Bishop (1787–1856). He was the first musician to be knighted and was also a professor of music at Oxford. His first operatic work was performed when he was 18. An inscription speaks of the 'grateful remembrance of the delight received by his admirers'.

Further off to the right of the mausoleum, nearer to the Dissenter's chapel and railinged on an island, is the extraordinary sarcophagus erected for Thomas Skarratt Hall (1836–1903) who made his fortune in mining in Australia. His burial place is in the style of Napoleon's tomb in Les Invalides. Angels once stood guard at each corner until they were stolen in 1989. Like the mausoleum, this appears more overwhelming than it might otherwise be because of the modest surroundings in which it has been placed and the scarcity of spectacular monuments. Designed by Sir Edwin Lutyens with a Latin inscription, the sarcophagus is red granite on a grey granite base.

By contrast to the grandiose memorials to Glenesk, Russell and Skarratt Hall, whose names are forgotten today, the British-born, naturalised American conductor, Leopold Stokowski (1882–1977), has a small, modest but elegant stone on a grave covered in newly blooming daffodils. The stone is engraved with the words: 'Music is the Voice of All'. It is to be found on East Avenue just past its junction with Rosemary Avenue.

Also in contrast to those spectacular monuments is the large but simple cross, down West Avenue from the chapel, where Harootune Nishan Mosditchian (1865–1919) rests. Whatever else he may have been, we are told he was 'a most noble and gallant gentleman'.

For pathos there is the grave of the three little Pettit girls, who died aged one hour, eight hours and 11 weeks, and who share the plot with someone, whom one presumes to be their grandfather, who died at the age of 94 in 2003.

As in Finchley Cemetery (see page 56), there are burial chambers – 32 of them in two rows with a double one set aside. However, unlike in the vast acres of Finchley, they are especially noticeable in the much smaller area here, even obtrusive: the bright stone stands out among the lush green of the surroundings, especially as they have been built on a small mound.

Some MPs have been laid to rest here. There is James Galloway Weir (1839–1911), Liberal MP for Ross and Cromarty and later Progressive party member of the London County Council. He and his family are in a large, roofed table tomb. Just to the right of the entrance is the grave of Sir James Boyton (1855–1926), MP for East Marylebone with his wife and their son, who perished on The Somme. There are rams heads at each top corner of the tomb with a wreath hanging between them.

The grave of the most distinguished parliamentarian here is that of Sir Austen Chamberlain (1863–1937), member of the War Cabinet in the First World War, chancellor of the exchequer, foreign secretary, Liberal Unionist MP, Conservative party leader, Nobel Prize winner, and half brother of Neville Chamberlain, who became prime minister in the year of Austen's death. The grave has a simple scroll, with a coat of arms on the headstone, and a pavement, and is toward the end of Central Avenue.

On this same row rests someone of a very different calling. Thomas Huxley (1825–1895) was a scientist and defender of Darwin and the person who coined the term 'agnostic'. Whoever inscribed his simple stone was not agnostic about the fact that 'God still giveth his beloved sleep'.

A recent show business personality to be found here is that of Melanie Appleby (1966–1990), who with her sister, Kim, formed Mel and Kim, a chart-topping singing duo. She died of pneumonia, at the age of 23, her immune system weakened by the chemotherapy she underwent for terminal cancer. Hers is a white marble grave, with scrolls, and a bed of blue stones. Harry Relf (1867–1928) was also in show business. He was better known as 'Little Titch', the music hall comedian and pantomime dame. In between these two, in the era of light entertainment, is Jimmy Nervo (1897–1975). With his partner Jimmy Knox (Nervo and Knox), he was an original member of the Crazy Gang.

There are numerous members of the newspaper-owning and political Harmsworth family buried at Finchley. The graves of the two most famous members are close to one another. They are the brothers, Alfred Harmsworth, Lord Northcliffe (1865–1922), founder of the *Daily Mail* and owner of *The Times*, and Harold Harmsworth, Lord Rothermere (1868–

1940), the fascist sympathiser who was well established as a newspaper proprietor when he acquired Associated Newspapers, owners of the *Daily Mail*, on his brother's death.

On Cypress Avenue, New York-born Henry Dwight Ripley (1864–1913) has a robed woman standing above the granite base of his grave, her head bowed in mourning. Even more impressive across the way is the verdigris-covered bronze Renaissance-style tomb of Thomas Tate (1832–1909) and his widow by three weeks, Esther (1837–1909). Here a stricken youth falls back, a finger pointed skywards.

Not far from the Tate's tomb and almost next to that of the Boytons, in a pleasantly shaded spot at the top of West Avenue, is a simple, black granite stone with gold lettering and a bed covered in green stones. PC Keith Blakelock (1945–1985) rests here, who was murdered in the Broadwater Farm riots in Tottenham.

East Finchley was created in 1854 but makes no claims to rival its great contemporaries, either in the number of distinguished residents or the magnificence or quantity of its monuments. However, it is just this modesty, combined with the delight of its landscape and its quiet and calm – along with the fact that many interesting people and memorials are here – that gives this an honoured place among London's cemeteries.

Getting there
East Finchley tube

Friends' association
No

Tours
No

Take a break
Dan and Decarlo, 20 High Road N2

Something else to see
Phoenix Cinema, High Road N2

Finchley (St Pancras and Islington) Cemetery

High Road N2

This is London's first publicly owned cemetery, created in 1854, and of all London's cemeteries it is the one that has the feel of being, literally, a city of the dead. The St Pancras Burial Board purchased 87 acres of farmland on Finchley Common, and a quarter of a century later another 94 acres were added. The first burial was to be followed by another 365,000 as the century turned and today it is estimated that nearly a million people are buried here. That includes 850,000 people whose first resting place is here and another 56,000 reinterments from London churchyards.

Strictly speaking, there are two cemeteries. Indistinguishable and with no dividing walls or hedges, the north western and south eastern parts are owned and managed by Islington Council. They are divided by the swathes of graves in south western and north eastern parts, which are looked after by Camden Council.

The municipal origins and present ownership are apparent: this is a largely well-kept cemetery, a funerary park, where, for the most part but not entirely, nature has been kept in its place. There are few places that are difficult to reach, woodland is sparse, and there are no great swathes of undergrowth to conjure up hidden worlds.

While this is very much well-planted parkland, its status as a necropolis comes partly from its size and layout, which are suggestive of a city – the long, tarmaced, well-maintained roads run off into the far distance. It is also urban-like because these roads are named as in a city – St Patrick's, St Peter's and St Paul's Avenues, Roman Road (named perhaps in deference to the large Catholic sections that they intersect), Middle Road, Circular Avenue, Parker's Road, High View Road, and so on. Like a city, street naming is redolent of a rural past before the bricks and mortar blotted it out: Harwood Path, Strawberry Vale Brook, and Stroud's Path.

The 10-minute walk to the bland office to obtain a site map takes one past what is now called the Islington Chapel, which is, in fact, a Decorated Gothic Anglican Church, with a 100-foot spire. This is now closed and seems to be used for storage, with two public toilets built into the sides. Burial services now take place at the red brick, squat St Pancras Chapel (once called the Episcopal Chapel) behind the second cemetery office, and committals are at the crematorium, thickly enclosed by trees, far off to the south east. The Dissenter's Chapel was demolished after the Second World War and the Catholic Chapel met a similar fate in 2009: only a grassy open space remains on Roman Road.

A great advantage for the visitor is again that, like a city, all the roads are clearly signposted. Thus, with the help of the site map it is easy to find one's way about. The disadvantage is that while the map clearly marks sections by cross referencing, no graves, significant or otherwise, are marked, and for an unaccountable reason the Camden south western section of the map contains road names but no plot numbers.

Despite this being a park, the cemetery is not without its rural elements: there are plenty of pleasant paths, lined by trees and undergrowth, to walk off the main roads, and off these are half-hidden stones, fallen monuments, and broken memorials. The main roads in the older parts of the cemetery – especially Viaduct Road – have a more rural feel about them than the more urban-like modern roads, for example, Lygoe Road.

While there are great tracts given over to new graves, there are also large areas where ancient and new can be found together. There are few of the spectacular memorials that one finds in, say, Highgate or West Norwood, but there are fine examples of Victorian and Edwardian sepulchral art.

Most of the mausoleums are unnoteworthy, small and unattractive, even nondescript. However, there is one of interest at the front of the site of the Catholic chapel (there is one at the back, too, but of little interest). It has gold leaf mosaic along the front at the top above a rusted iron gate. Built by Gaetano Melesi, it commemorates the person who was presumably his wife, Letizia Melesi, who died in January 1914 when hit by a taxi in Holborn. We can assume that hers is the prostrate figure shown on a panel.

There may be a dearth of spectacular memorials, but nonetheless there are plenty of tombs, columns, decorated crosses, and obelisks – good examples come almost immediately in view if one walks the Circular Road from the main entrance – which taken together are well worth seeing. There are also interesting individual graves to seek out, such as the Dean grave on Viaduct Road, which contains eight members of that family. It has a marble base on which a life-sized angel stands with a wreath in one hand, while the other rests on a rough-edged headstone.

The most notable monument in the cemetery is the Grade II listed Mond mausoleum on Chapel Hill, which is set on a tree-shaded small slope. It was designed by Thomas Arthur Darcy Braddell in the Greek style (based on the Temple of Nemesis) in granite and Portland stone, with a pediment supported by two fluted Ionic columns. It commemorates Ludwig Mond

(1839–1909), the inventor of alloy nickel and a German-born chemist, industrialist and philanthropist. It was built by his two sons, Sir Robert and Sir Alfred (the latter, the first Lord Melchett). Melchett (1868–1930), the creator of the industrial conglomerate ICI, sometime Liberal Cabinet Minister and later Conservative MP, is buried here, as is his grandson, Julian, the third Lord Melchett (1925–1973), another industrialist.

HERE LIE THE REMAINS
OF
MEN AND WOMEN
ONCE LAID TO REST IN
ST. PANCRAS CHURCHYARD
WHICH WERE REINTERRED IN
ST. PANCRAS CEMETERY IN 2003
DURING CONSTRUCTION OF THE
CHANNEL TUNNEL RAIL LINK.
THEIR NAMES ARE UNKNOWN BUT
THEIR MEMORY IS TREASURED.
MAY THEY REST IN PEACE.

However, usually unnoted is another equally striking mausoleum, the more curious as it is prominently positioned on the corner of Roman Road and Lygoe Road. This is the burial place of the Stacchini family. It is a 12-foot high, white marble box, with an incongruous, somewhat shabby wooden door. The memorial lacks any inscription or decoration, except for the engraved family name and a tiny engraving of a boy tipping water from a container.

There are several areas devoted to the graves of babies and young people, but one of the most poignant areas is on Viaduct Road where former residents of Arlington House, the hostel for homeless men in Camden Town, are buried. The Arlington House Irish Association erected a memorial to those buried here and to Sir Richard Farrant, the chair of Rowton House (who is buried in West Sussex). It has an inscription from Patrick Kavanagh's autobiography, *The Green Fool*: 'Many Irish boys made Rowton (Arlington) House, Camden Town, first stop from Mayo ... the soft voices of Mayo and Galway, sounded in that gaunt, impersonal place fell like warm rain on the arid patches of my imagination.'

To judge by their often advanced ages, Arlington House became the first and final stop for many of these men. They rest in graves only marked by a wooden cross and a brass plate giving their names and dates, spread around a grassy, unkempt field. The number of crosses close together suggests that these may well be common graves.

Nearby, at the back of the field, is a simple oval stone that marks the resting place of remains disinterred in 2003 from Old St Pancras Churchyard (see page 104) for the building of the Channel Tunnel rail link. Of these men and women we are told 'their names are unknown but their memory is treasured. May they rest in peace'.

This was, however, not the first reinterment here caused by the needs of the development of the city. There are two areas where the remains rest of those who were originally buried in the churchyard of St Mary's Church, Islington, and were taken to the cemetery to allow the widening of Upper Street in both 1865 and 1883. Also, reburied here are the remains of those from St Luke's Church, Old Street, Shoreditch.

The cemetery is especially notable for a very large number of attractive modern headstones. One sees these, collectively, at their best by standing on the corner of New Road and Joint Road and looking across to where the area looks like a sea of black and white marble headstones, broken by the blues, reds and yellows of flowers (albeit many artificial). It has to be said, too, that by the time one has got this far, the birdsong is drowned out by the roar of the traffic on the North Circular Road that skirts the northern side of the cemetery.

One funerary innovation is the so-called 'burial chambers', which apparently have been requested by various communities (largely by Italians to judge by the minority that have been taken) in the last decade or so. (They can also be found in New Southgate Cemetery (see And elsewhere ... page 144), nearby East Finchley Cemetery (see page 50), and Wolves Lane Cemetery, Haringey.) Built of a concrete mix, which looks like sandstone, with granite additions and coverings, they have metal plaques ready for inscription, and are perfectly lined up in Church Avenue. The chambers offer an eerie feeling that they have been built for use after some future disaster.

Some very good examples of memorials of the last 30 to 40 years – which are built in a much more traditional, occasionally ornate style – are those that belong, among others, to the Francies, Connell, Agius, Dobson, Berni, Brazoli, Solari, Cavaciuti, Cunnane and Skibrinski families. These line the road opposite the Stacchini mausoleum. Here are good examples of broad bases, with often a black marble headstone, adorned with traditional Catholic statuary.

Finchley also has some curiosities like the grave of William French, who died on 13 July 1896 when he saved a dog from drowning in Highgate Ponds. Public subscription paid for a memorial that has the statue of a dog, which may be the one he saved, sitting on the base. Also, Spencer Percival (1864–1913) was a balloonist, cyclist and gymnast. His uncle George Spencer (died 1916), who introduced the velocipede (or bicycle) to England from France in 1868 is also buried in Finchley in a grave just off Junction Path, which has been recently refurbished. The short column on his grave used to have a balloon on it, but after being stolen, another is presently in storage for the family. There is an engraved parachute on the grave of 'Captain' Alfred Smith (died 1914), which he shares with Harry Gardener (died aged 48 in 1917), a clown well known at the Lyceum Theatre in London. The balloonist is commonly assumed to be Gardener but in fact, Smith – his title was assumed for professional purposes – was with his wife 'Countess S', also a balloonist.

What the cemetery lacks in ornate or spectacular monuments, it makes up for in the variety of those buried here and its sense of space, openness and calm.

Getting there
East Finchley tube

Friends' association
No

Tours
No

Take a break
Café at the Phoenix Cinema, 52 High Road N2

Something else to see
Black Gull Bookshop, 121 High Road N2

Gardens of Peace Muslim Cemetery

Elmbridge Road, Hainault

The Gardens of Peace Muslim Cemetery – far out in London's most easterly borough – is like no other. It is London's newest cemetery (opened in 2002), one of only two Muslim cemeteries in London, and, at 51.5 acres, the largest in Europe.

However, what strikes the visitor immediately about the cemetery is its uniformity. There are no memorials or religious imagery and few flowers. All the graves are exactly the same: body length humps of what, at first sight, looks like rough concrete but is in fact a soil natural to the area. All graves point to the east in the direction of Mecca (a position not always achieved when Muslims are buried elsewhere). At the head of each grave is a foot-square, flat, marble stone – some in white, most in grey (the original white was abandoned due to claims of glare in the sun) – each with an inscription in the same style: the name of the deceased and below that the date of death according to the Gregorian and Islamic calendars. This arrangement is based on equality under Allah: rich and poor, the better known and those known only to friends and relatives, are indistinguishable.

Planted equidistantly along the rows between the graves are semi-mature trees. Low hedges separate sections and there are plenty of seats, as well as a designated area for sitting and contemplation.

There are no family graves, which, from a religious perspective, are only permitted where there is a shortage of space. Neither can plots be reserved. Scholarly opinion states that this should not be done as one does not know where or when one is going to die and it is always best to be buried where one has died.

A stream pleasantly traverses the northern side of the cemetery. This is a cemetery, which, with its ranked uniformity, has the quiet dignity (indeed, in some ways, even the look) of a military cemetery.

There are signs that warn against the laying of flowers. This has no religious value, they say, and 'is only for personal gratification', and they go on to state that the dead only benefit by 'pious acts': *dua* (prayers or, more correctly, supplication), charity, and the distribution of Islamic literature.

There is a simple beauty to these graves, row after row, set amid rich green grass. Yet closer up and at an angle, with the grass out of the line of vision, the impression is of undulating earth – or even the desert – seen from a great distance above. There is also a great sense of spaciousness, caused by the

lack of broad trunks and rich foliage of oaks and beech, towering memorials, and bends and slopes that often characterise other cemeteries. One comes through the metal gate and is able to take in the whole expanse of the place. Immediately to the left through the gate, by the office, is the women's prayer room; further on is one for men near the large Hall of Remembrance, which was completed in 2011. This includes facilities for *wudhu* (ritual washing before prayer) and contemplation. Taps are provided on entry to the cemetery so that mud brought in on shoes does not mark the paths.

Men and women are buried together in five sections. The first is for those who died at less than 17 weeks (foetuses), where graves are unmarked and not necessarily maintained. Then there is the section for those who have died aged 17 weeks and over (still births); those aged zero to two; two to 12; and last those aged 12 and over (adults).

The use of the humped shaped grave is a reminder of the omnipresence of the camel in Arab lands at the time of the Prophet Mohammed. But it is not just that symbolism and the fact of the graves facing east that makes this a distinctively Muslim cemetery. The trees and shrubs – olive, palm and fig trees, and rose bushes – are all those mentioned in the Koran.

The Gardens of Peace Muslim Cemetery is owned and run by a charity and was paid for largely by *qardh husanah* (interest-free loans). It has received three awards: for total concept design, land renewal and landscaping. Twenty and a half acres of the present site allows for a capacity for 10,000 burials. Much of this land is, as yet, unused, but grass has been sown on all of it and trees planted in preparation for future interments. An additional 30 acres was purchased in 2007 but most of this will be largely used for woodland and a nature reserve.

Most Muslims are buried in municipal cemeteries, either in usually small sections, where others of their faith rest, or among other non-Muslim graves.

London's only other Muslim cemetery, The Waltham Forest Cemetery Trust, only serves that borough. The Gardens of Peace was originally only intended to be for Muslims in east London, but demand has been such from all parts of the capital that this is now the resting place for any Muslim Londoner.

Janazah (funerals) take place 24 hours after death with the deceased buried in a shroud, not a coffin, according to custom. Funerals can be carried out 365 days a year but the cemetery is closed between 12.30pm and 2pm on Fridays for *jumu'ah* (Friday prayers).

One of the most significant and tragic of burials here was on 15 July 2005. Large numbers of people came to the cemetery when Shahara Islam was laid to rest. The 20-year-old, east London-born bank cashier was murdered in the London bombings when travelling on the No. 30 bus. (It is said that 7,000 people attended the funeral service at the mosque.) However, the largest numbers to attend a burial also occurred because of another terrible tragedy: 1,000 people came when Muna Kua and her five children were buried. They had lost their lives in a fire at their house in Neasden.

A journey out toward the end of the Central line makes this a very worthwhile visit, not only as an education for the non-Muslim but, despite the steady hum of traffic, this cemetery is well named: here one experiences a serenity that lends itself to contemplation.

Getting there
Hainault tube station

Friends' association
No

Tours
No

Take a break
The Station Café, 206 New North Road, Hainault

Something else to see
Nothing

Hampstead Cemetery

Fortune Green Road NW6

While a time traveller transported to the present day would be shocked by the traffic edging along Fortune Green Road, standing at the gates of Hampstead Cemetery, he or she would nevertheless recognise the place for what it was when it opened in 1876.

The twin chapels, united by a cloche de porter, can still be seen in the distance separating the upper half from the lower half of the cemetery. The railings, the stone gateposts and the Gothic lodge at the entrance have not been destroyed or replaced, as in too many cemeteries (the railings were taken away during the Second World War but were later restored).

Once through the gates, the change is self-evident: this is no longer the largely empty space that early prints depict: 60,000 people have come to rest here in those 137 years. The cemetery was founded when the parish churchyard of St John at Hampstead (see page 110) became overcrowded. However, unlike others that bear the name of their geographical location but are not within that area – for example, Paddington, Islington and St Pancras, and St Marylebone – Hampstead Cemetery is still in the same borough and only a mile or so from its 'mother' burial ground.

There are a large number of mature ash trees, together with yew, sycamore, Norway maple, silver birch, Lombardy poplar, purple cherry-plum, willow and Swedish white beam. As is common now in cemeteries, a wildlife area has been created – here, it is in the northern part of the eastern half – that has been planted with trees, shrubs and wildflowers. Among them are field maple, hazel, oak, oxeye daisy, common knapweed, and bird's-foot-trefoil, and it is here where most of the site's butterflies are to be found.

Being Hampstead, the cemetery has attracted interments of the rich and the eccentric (sometimes one and the same), those who have excelled in their fields, as well as many local worthies. And being Hampstead and its environs, too, those buried here come from many backgrounds. Hardly through the gates, one is struck by the number of Irish and Arabic names on headstones that are fairly recent burials. The number of Irish, which proliferate the deeper one goes into the cemetery, may perhaps be accounted for by the proximity of Kilburn, with its large Irish population. The further one proceeds, one also comes across large numbers of Poles, Italians and Spanish who rest here, together with some Chinese and at least one Romanian. In the south west corner, there are a number of Celtic crosses, which account for a large Scots contingent.

One of the largest – but otherwise unremarkable tombs – where someone from overseas has their last resting place is in section A (the cemetery is divided into sections from A to D), immediately before the gate through the railinged footpath that divides the 26 acres. This is the tomb of Grand Duke Michael Michailovitch (1861–1929), grandson of Tsar Nicholas I of Russia, and the Grand Duke's wife, Countess Torby (1868–1927), granddaughter of the poet Pushkin. The couple secretly and morganatically married in 1891, thus alienating many Romanov relatives, and were forced into exile.

Managed by the London Borough of Camden, Hampstead is a largely well-kept cemetery: its main paths are unobstructed; its grass kept in check; comparatively few graves are lost to ivy or undergrowth; and comparatively few are broken or fallen.

It rests on a very slight incline that runs down on one side to a playing field, so a visitor is likely to be accompanied less by bird song (although several species of bird are to be found here) and more by the shouts of children and others indulging in a game being played on the other side of the fence. The cemetery has no new grave spaces available, but there is an area for cremated remains to the north of the cemetery.

There are two Gothic-style chapels, which are Grade II listed buildings, as is the lodge, which is made of Kentish Rag and Bath stone. The three buildings were designed by Charles Bell (died 1899) who is buried here. Lottery funding has improved the buildings, roads and landscaping. Only the southern chapel is used for inter-denominational worship.

Three particularly notable monuments stand not far from one another close to the main entrance. The first is the art deco, triangular-shaped Bianchi monument, which has a large angel, wings raised, above the grave itself. This was created by Cesare Bianchi, chef de cuisine at the Café Royal, for his wife, Mattie (Martha), who died in 1936 soon after the birth of their son. Either side of the grave are two stone panels. One shows the couple with their baby and the other shows Mattie ascending into heaven. Built in Italy, the memorial was shipped to this country in pieces and assembled on site. The small metal entry gate has gone and the walls at the sides have lost their railings. Cesare himself met a tragic end when he and his sister-in-law Mary, who had come to London to look after the children, died in March 1945 when a V2 rocket fell near Smithfield Market in one of the last air raids on London.

Not far away from these monuments is the life-sized stone church organ, with sculpted stops, pipes and sheet music, which sits on the grave of Charles Barritt (died 1929), a London publican who is also believed to have been an entertainer. The stall was at one time stolen but has now been replaced. (Hampstead seems especially prone to the stealing of some of its most notable memorials: the bronze urn was removed from the Frankau monument in 1997. The life-size bronze of a robed woman by the sculptor Sir William Goscombe John (1860–1952) to his wife, Marthe (died 1923), has been removed, leaving a now dreary, grey upright structure.)

The third especially noteworthy memorial nearby is that of the architect Banister Fletcher (1833–1899). Four columns hold a canopy on which rests an urn on a cenotaph with two robed women seated below. The bust beneath is said to have been removed by someone who appeared before Banister in court in his capacity as a magistrate. The monument commemorates not only Fletcher, his wife Eliza Jane (1847–1933) and their son, Sir Banister Flight Fletcher, architect and barrister, but no less than eight other family members.

James Wilson (1875–1901), known as 'pasha' as his inscription shows, was chief engineer to the Egyptian government. Appropriately, his comparatively small but impressive chest tomb, in red marble, has three columns each side with Egyptian motifs, and looks like an Egyptian temple.

By contrast to such grandiosity, Sir Joseph (later Lord) Lister (1827–1912), pioneer of antiseptic surgery, refused the offer of burial in Westminster Abbey, and rests beneath a modest, three-step stone in grey marble.

Charles James Fuller (died 1891), founder and vicar of St Mary's, Primrose Hill and follower of the Anglo-Catholic Oxford Movement, has an impressive neo-Gothic table tomb, but how John Kensit (1853–1902) would have felt about resting not far away we can only guess. He founded the Protestant Truth Society and fought strongly against the ritualism beloved by Fuller and his colleagues. The inscription on Kensit's obelisk, erected by the London Council of United Protestant Societies but now with large stones strewn about its base, says that he was 'raised in God to defend the Protestant faith and the liberties secured at the blessed Reformation'. It also tells us that he was 'a martyr in the cause of Christ' who was 'struck down by the missile of an assassin'. In truth, this man, described in the *Oxford Dictionary of National Biography* as a 'sincere but narrow-minded fanatic', was struck by a chisel thrown by a member of a crowd he was preaching to, and while Kensit was taken to hospital, he recovered from his injury but died of pneumonia.

Probably the best known of the businessmen buried here is the Italian-born Charles (later Lord) Forte (1908–2007), with his wife, Irene (1921–2010). His headstone refers to him as a 'philanthropist' and 'great patriarch' as if he were an Old Testament prophet rather than a caterer and hotelier, of which the inscription also reminds us. He lies across the path from two other large and attractive Forte family graves that contain his parents and other relatives. Frank Debenham (died 1917), chairman of the store that bears his family's name, lies behind Charles Forte. Elsewhere in the cemetery is a name once famous in north London but whose store has long gone: Thomas Bowman (died 1905). Even Forte's empire – including the Waldorf, budget hotels, restaurants, and the Café Royal, which once employed 68,000 people – has now shrivelled to a few luxury hotels run by his son, Sir Rocco.

Forte might be intrigued to know that his grave is next to that of Victoria Modupe 'Chief' Smith (1937–1984), where there is a fine bas-relief of her in profile on the head stone and what may be the only inscription in Yoruba in the UK. This describes her as 'market woman of Ago Oko and Egba Okeona, Chief of Ikija and successful business woman of Ido Ekiti'. Given the latter, maybe she and her companion in death would have had something in common after all. As for inscriptions, where else is there one in shorthand as there is on the not-easy-to-find grave of Louisa Day (died 1905)?

Close to Forte, Smith and Debenham also rests Mordant Allen Gwynne (died 1910), whose splendid name and extravagant tomb – a pedestal supporting two winged and robed angels – are at variance with the fact that we know nothing about him.

Being Hampstead there is a good smattering of graves and memorials to those in the theatrical profession. Among them is Dame Gladys Cooper (1888–1971), who worked into her 82nd year. Her grave is at the extreme right of the footpath not far from the playing ground fence. Her one time father-in-law, the newspaper magnate and founder of St Dunstan's, Sir Arthur Pearson, has his own very impressive memorial near the entrance where two main paths meet to the right of the lodge and the central avenue.

From the theatre, too, are the comedian Ronald Fraser (1930–1997), whose simple stone has an unacknowledged poem by Sir Noel Coward; the actor Clive Brook (1887–1974); Sir Charles Wyndham (1837–1919), the actor-manager and his actress wife, Mary Moore (1861–1931); and Fred Terry (1863–1933), Shakespearean actor, brother of the more famous Ellen, and his wife, the actress Julia Neilson (1868–1957). There are also those from a less elevated aspect of that profession, the music hall, notably Marie Lloyd (1870–1922), whose funeral, said to have been watched by 50,000 people, is still the largest to which the cemetery has been host. Her grave is on the path to the left of that of Sir Arthur Pearson.

Across the path from Sir Arthur Pearson, the novelist Nigel Balchin (1908–1970) has a headstone in the shape of a book that bears his inscription and the words 'Lord, I was afraid', which is the title of his novel published in 1947. In this area, too, Ernest Raymond (1888–1974) also takes the title of one of his books – *Good Morning, Good People* – as an inscription. The humorist and writer Alan Coren (1938–2007) has Mr Punch (he wrote for the magazine) engraved on his simple headstone and the words: 'Tomorrow to fresh woods and crinkles new'. This is a final thrust of his reference to the local area as 'Crinklewood', much to its residents' annoyance. The Australian-born war correspondent and historian Alan Moorehead (1910–1983) and the author and illustrator Kate Greenaway (1846–1901) are also among the literary society gathered in section D. Along the path from Pearson rests Andrew Fisher (1862–1928), a Scottish-born pit boy who became Labour prime minister of Australia.

There cannot be many cemeteries where not just one, but two Nobel Prize winners rest. Sir William Randal Creamer (1838–1908), an MP and trades unionist, is half way up the path running parallel on the right once at the twin chapels. He is almost forgotten now, but he won the prize for peace in 1903 and gave most of the £7,000 prize money to the International Arbitration League. Sir Joseph Rotblat (1908–2005), the nuclear physicist, is a fellow laureate. His inscription, 'Above all, remember your humanity', appears to be based on a saying of fellow peace activist and Nobel Prize winner (for literature), Bertrand Russell, who wrote: 'Remember your humanity and forget the rest'.

Up the path from Marie Lloyd, the former MP and TUC president Sir Tom O'Brien (1900–1970) has a grave edged by hedges. Curiously, the inscription, 'Only the actions of the just/Smell sweet and blossom in their dust' from James Shirley's lines, sometimes called 'Death the leveller' substitutes 'great' for 'just'. The rhyme may be lost but we must hope this is error and not egotism.

At the bottom of that path is the grave of Charles Cowper Ross (1929–1985), whose headstone calls him 'a man of the theatre' (he was a theatrical producer, director and actor). His inscription stands in sharp contrast to that of O'Brien. Like all cemeteries, so many of those buried here were famous in their day but forgotten now, and Cowper Ross's epitaph counsels humility:

'What will be said,
When I am dead,
Of what I used to do?
They liked my smile?
I failed with style?
Or, more than likely, "Who?"'

Getting there
West Hampstead tube station, West Hampstead rail station, West Hampstead Thameslink, and Cricklewood Station

Friends' association
Yes

Tours
No

Take a break
David's Deli, 341 West End Lane NW6

Something else to see
Freud Museum, 20 Maresfield Gardens NW3

Highgate (St James) Cemetery

Swain's Lane N6

There may well be 'many things to be heard and seen before we get to Paradise by way of Kensal Green', if GK Chesterton was right, but there are enough things worth seeing without even going beyond the walls of Kensal Green Cemetery. This is not just the first of the great Victorian Cemeteries to be created in 1833, but perhaps the most remarkable of all of the Magnificent Seven in terms of its architecture, tombs and who is buried here. This is the aristocrat of cemeteries – proud, unbowed despite difficult times, which endows those whom it shelters as much as they endow it. It has also been termed 'The Belgravia of Death'.

Striking, even elegant as Kensal Green may be as a cemetery, it is a haven of quiet in an unprepossessing part of northwest London (the main road to the north is not obtrusive and the Grand Union Canal is to the south). It embraces two conservation areas and is home to 33 species of bird and other wildlife, encouraged by areas thick with trees. Its tree-lined paths are quiet and well kept, and most graves are well spaced and easy to reach, although some of the memorials are fallen and broken. While there are large sections of new graves, many new graves sit companionably with much older ones. Just as neighbouring St Mary's Roman Catholic Cemetery (see page 116) was created from land purchased from Kensal Green, so a Greek Orthodox Cemetery, consecrated in 2005, has been created in the same way.

After a shaky start, it was a post-mortem royal patronage that established not only the cemetery's attraction as a burial place, but also the kind of people who often wished to be buried there. Augustus Frederick, Duke of Sussex (1773–1843), son of George III and uncle of Queen Victoria, chose Kensal Green because he did not want to be buried in 'that stinking hole' – St George's Chapel, Windsor – after he had witnessed his brother, William IV, laid to rest there, with (it was said) not a tear shed, chattering and sniggering, and a long and tedious service. The duke's funeral, on 6 April 1843, was a lavish one. He is buried with his wife, Celia Underwood, the Duchess of Inverness (c 1785–1873), whom he married morganatically. Theirs is a very large Cornish grey slab, surrounded by pineapple bollards. Five years later the duke's sister, Princess Sophia (1777–1848), was buried across the Central Avenue. She was buried in front of the Anglican chapel, in a vault beneath a white Carrara marble sarcophagus monument that stands on a large podium of stone on a base of grey Cornish granite. It was designed by Lüdwig Gruner, Prince Albert's architect.

Fifty-six years after Sophia's interment, her nephew Prince George, the Duke of Cambridge (1819–1904), was deposited in his Egyptian mausoleum, where he joined his wife, Sarah Fairbrother (1816–1890), an actress, singer and male impersonator. She was the mother of two when they met and the widow of a man who was not the father of either of her children. She had two children with the duke before they married and then a child born in wedlock. The Duke's mistress, Mrs Louisa Beauclerk ('the idol of my life and my existence') lies 20 yards away. Disgruntled at being forced to resign after 39 years as commander-in-chief of the army (a nepotistic appointment by his cousin, Queen Victoria), his coffin is inscribed to say that he held the post for 'nearly 40 years'.

The Duke of Sussex's decision paid off for the cemetery: by 1850 it was said to be the only one of its kind yielding a good dividend. The General Cemetery Company is still the owner, making this the only cemetery in London to remain in private ownership. The Company was inspired by barrister George Frederick Carden (1798–1874), who had visited Père Lachaise and is buried at Kensal Green just south of Princess Sophia. The Company had been formed two years before the cemetery opened, but it took the city's first outbreak of cholera in 1832 to overcome resistance to non-church burials. An Act of Parliament empowered it to create Kensal Green.

The company had paid £9,500 paid for 54 acres, 48 of which were consecrated acres and seven left unconsecrated for Dissenters. It was laid out as a garden cemetery and was planted in the manner of Paris's Père Lachaise. Another 22 acres were later acquired to the west and land to the west was later sold to the Catholic Church to create St Mary's Roman Catholic Cemetery.

One hundred guineas were offered as the prize in a design competition, with a budget of £10,000 for the chapel and £3,000 for the gateway. Forty-eight sets of plans were submitted, but the choice was made more complicated by 'The Battle of the Styles' – Neo-classical versus Gothic Revival – a struggle epitomised by the near contemporaneous building of the Palace of Westminster and the National Gallery. Henry Edward Kendall won the competition with his Gothic Revival design. However, anti-Catholic feeling at the time caused this to be rejected because of the style's association with 'popery', which, it was felt, would offend the potential customers from the Anglican middle classes.

John Griffith was made chief architect and his Greek Revival designs won the day, with Richard Forrest, former head gardener of Syon Park, designing the landscape. Griffith's chapels (Doric for the Anglican, Ionic for Dissenters), gateway and lodge adorned the cemetery five years after the

opening. The handsome Doric Gateway in Harrow Road, with its triumphal arch is yet nothing next to the neo-classical chapel that dominates the centre of the cemetery. The interior of this Grade I listed building, which is now in a poor state of repair with dry rot and exposed brick work – but with a hope of renovation – seems disproportionately small compared to the exterior, with its soaring porticoed façade and spreading, L-shaped, colonnaded wings.

The chapel and the space outside sit above a catacomb that has space for 4,000 coffins (1,000 of the 4,000 loculi are still available). The chapel has one of the only three working hydraulic coffin lifts in the UK (one is in St George's Chapel, Windsor, and the other is next door in St Mary's). This allows the coffins to descend from the catafalque to the catacombs. (There are two other catacombs at Kensal Green – one beneath the Dissenters' Chapel – but they cannot be visited and those beneath the chapel can only be seen as part of one of the Friends' frequent guided tours.)

Among those placed down below is the Earl of Mornington (1788–1857), a gambler, womaniser, general reprobate, sometime MP, and nephew of the Duke of Wellington. His coffin today would cost about £20,000, with its crest of a noble coronet, velvet covering and silver studs. This was no small achievement for a man upon whose death shopkeepers rejoiced so that they could cash in the insurance policies they had taken out against what he owed them.

However, the Gothic style, banished from the overall design, is far from absent in the commemorations of many of those buried here. There is the polychrome Gothic mausoleum that the architect John Gibson (1817–1892) designed for himself. He also created a massive octagonal mausoleum (1864) for the Molyneaux family that combines Carrara marble, Peterhead granite and Rubishaw granite. General Sir William Casement (1780–1844) had himself remembered with a classical monument on the south side of Central Avenue, redolent of his time as member of the Council of India. This is a sarcophagus, with a ceremonial military headdress resting on top, sitting on a Portland stone base, with four robed bowed telemones (or male caryatids) dressed as servants of the Indian Raj, holding a canopy on their up stretched hands.

Sir Richard Mayne (1796–1868), the first joint commissioner of the Metropolitan Police (and, for 39 years, the longest serving), rests beneath a towering pink Peterhead granite obelisk. On South Avenue, the 14-foot marble spire of Feargus O'Connor (1794–1855), MP, orator and Chartist is also quite imposing. O'Connor's inscription reads: 'While philanthropy is a virtue and patriotism not a crime will the name of O'Connor be admired and this monument respected'.

Others of eccentric callings are to be found here, as well as many in the arts and sciences. One who, by his inscription, considered himself somewhat dubiously a friend of both was Andrew Ducrow (1793–1842). The fashion for the Egyptian style can be seen with the £3,000 that his mausoleum cost him. He was a showman and circus performer who wrestled with lions and who, it was said, could lift five children using only his teeth. He often referred to himself as the 'Father of British circus equestrianism' and 'the Colossus of Equestrians'. The mausoleum, which was created for his wife bears the inscription: 'This tomb is created by genius for the reception of its own remains', adding, with the same self-deprecation, that this was one 'whose death deprived the arts and sciences of an eminent professor and liberal patron'. However, his implied handiwork is false. The tomb is one of the largest and most decorated tombs within the cemetery in one of the most desirable plots (situated in the Central Avenue) and was designed by Ducrow's theatrical designer. The decoration is primarily pagan with sphinxes watching over the door. The tomb was originally brightly painted in pastel hues to attract the eye, but these have faded with time.

By contrast to such extravagance in stone, Harold Pinter (1930–2008) lies across the way from Ducrow, under a flat simple stone, just back from the pathway. The inscription refers to him as a playwright and Nobel laureate, but also husband of the historian, Antonia Fraser. Curiously, for a Jewish-born atheist, he is not only buried in Anglican-consecrated ground, but his death date is given not as 24 December 2008 but as 'Christmas Eve 2008'.
Jean-Francois Gravelet Blondin (1824–1897), who among other things, walked a tightrope several times in several different ways across the Niagara Falls, lies here with his wife Charlotte (who died, aged 52, in 1888). Their marble medallion portraits in profile are on the front of their tall, pink, Peterhead granite headstone on their double grave.

While Frederick Windsor (1763–1830), the pioneer of public gas lighting, is buried in Père Lachaise, his tall sandstone memorial is, alas, in a poor state of repair, but still worth looking at. It has two biblical passages, which seem to take biblical justification a step too far. 'At evening time it shall be light' says the passage from Zachariah, while St John might be surprised to find Christ's words, 'I am come, a light unto the world', used for this purpose.

The largest plot in the cemetery is to the south of the Anglican chapel. Here rests someone who was both noble and eccentric. Under a beech tree there is a large but simple granite stone on a two-step base surrounded by small pillars, from which the linking railing chains have been stolen. It is the grave of William John Cavendish-Bentinck-Scott, the 5th Duke of Portland (1800–1879). He was so reclusive that that he would have his carriage loaded on the train from Welbeck Abbey, his stately home in Nottinghamshire, so that he could then drive direct from the train to his London home. Dying childless, after his demise a Mrs Druce attempted to claim the Portland fortune (and the title for her son) by claiming that her late father-in-law and the Duke were one and the same and that Mr Druce's coffin had been filled with lead. Only exhumation of Mr Thomas Druce's coffin from Highgate Cemetery settled the matter and Mrs Druce ended her days in a lunatic asylum.

Thomas Hood (1799–1845), the poet, also rests here in a grave raised by public subscription, as befits one for whom debt came as readily as rhyme. A bust, once on top, has been stolen and the birth date on the inscription is given one year earlier than it actually was.

Percy Sholto Douglas, 10th Marquess of Queensbury (1868–1920), has a marble cross under a Gothic canopy. He disliked his father, John, the sporting and uncouth 9th marquess, as much as did his brother, Lord Alfred 'Bosie' Douglas, the lover of Oscar Wilde. It is apt, then, that Oscar's mother, Jane Francisca Agnes, Lady Wilde (1821–1896) should share the same burial ground as Bosie's brother and rests under a striking new headstone, which has been placed on what was her unmarked grave in a rather isolated spot. It refers to her as a 'writer, translator, poet, nationalist, early advocate of equality for women'. By a nice association with this cemetery's origins, Oscar is buried in Père Lachaise.

Another writer who is buried not far away under a white marble cross on a four-step base is George Grossmith (1847–1912). Although better known as the author of *The Diary of a Nobody* (1894) with his brother Weedon, George was also the first person to sing 'The Major-General's Song' from *The Pirates of Penzance*.

Charles Dickens' sister-in-law, Mary Hogarth (1819–1837) is buried in a grave that the novelist, in his still obscure relationship with her, wished one day to share. His biographer, John Forster (1817–1876) rests in a classical mausoleum, which is symbolic of the weight of his work. The loss to Westminster Abbey of Wilkie Collins (1824–1889), Dickens' friend and father of the detective novel, is Kensal Green's gain.

William Mulready (1786–1863), one of several Royal Academicians buried here, lies as a recumbent effigy beneath a canopy supported by six columns on a large base. Four sides have engraved representations of 15 of his paintings. This highly decorated tomb by Godfrey Sykes is in Pulhamite, an artificial stone.

Harriet Marian Stephen (1840–1875), first wife of Sir Leslie Stephen (who was Virginia Woolf and Vanessa Bell's father), does not lie near her father, the novelist William Makepeace Thackeray (1811–1863), who has a slab tomb with railings elsewhere in the cemetery. Instead, her companions in death are her brother-in-law, Sir James Fitzjames Stephen (1829–1894), a High Court judge, and her father-in-law, Sir James Stephen (1789–1859) each under a rounded white stone. It was Sir James who delivered a judgment that made cremation legal. He was known as 'Mr Over-Secretary' due to his over-bearing manner when Under-Secretary of State for the Colonies. However, in that capacity he ended the slave trade in those lands and became a professor of modern history at Cambridge.

In a white, attractive, comparatively plain grave rests Sir Marc Brunel (1769–1849), civil engineer and creator of the Thames Tunnel, along with several members of his family. These include his arguably more famous son, Isambard Kingdom Brunel (1806–1859), who was a ship designer and builder of 25 railways and five suspension bridges, including the Clifton Suspension Bridge.

The inscription (referring to Sir Marc but equally appropriate for Isambard) says that 'he raised his own monument by his public works'. This is reminiscent of that of Wren's in St Paul's Cathedral: 'Reader, if you seek a monument, look around you'. This can be said of George Frederick Carden, John Griffith of Finsbury, Richard Forrest and their associates, the creators of Kensal Green Cemetery.

Getting there
Kensal Green rail and tube stations

Friends' association
Yes

Tours
Yes

Take a break
Minkie's Deli, 'Glasshouse', Chamberlayne Road NW10

Something else to see
Brent Museum, 95 High Road NW10

Moravian
Burial Ground

King's Road SW10

The first person was laid to rest here in 1751 but the first I could find (because many of the stones are so weathered as to make the inscriptions indecipherable) was Benjamin La Trobe, who died aged 58 on 29 November 1786 (appropriate that he should be the first that one can find as his family has a long Moravian history stretching to the present day). He was followed a year later by the splendidly named John Renatus Charles (born in 1710). Another notable burial is that of James Gillray (1720–1799), sexton, and father of the cartoonist, James Gillray.

God's Acres are divided in four to allow the separate burial places for married and unmarried men and women, boys and girls. However, I found that John Frederick Pemsey (1832–1918) had managed to get himself next to his wife Eleanor Sophia in the women's section. Four fig trees in the centre of the burial field mark the four paths between the sections.

Today the congregation is 25 strong. As they come to their Sunday service they look across at the resting places of some of those who have ensured their Church's survival, from its origins in Moravia nearly 600 years ago to this small plot in affluent west London.

Getting there
Kensington High Street tube station

Friends' association
No

Tours
No

Take a break
Il Portico, 277 Kensington High Street W8

Something else to see
Thomas Carlyle's House, Cheyne Walk SW3

Nunhead (All Saints) Cemetery

Linden Grove SE15

Nothing can prepare the visitor for Nunhead Cemetery. The area is quiet, with no main road with buses, lorries and other traffic roaring by. Many Londoners would be hard put to say where Nunhead actually is, and even then 'near Peckham Rye' indicates that it lacks a readily recognised identity. Its railway station lies on one of those not very well known but very useful lines that criss-cross south London. The streets surrounding it are unremarkable and there are only a handful of shops near the station.

Like the area that surrounds it in south London, Nunhead does not blow its own trumpet, unlike Highgate Cemetery and its local area. Nunhead makes too much of its modesty, for here is the fifth of the Magnificent Seven. At 52 acres, it is the second largest, and was opened in 1840 by the same company that created Highgate, with which it shares a high aspect. It is possibly the least well known and maybe least visited, yet it is one of the most attractive and atmospheric of the Seven. Its long wall and railings overwhelm the small estates and terraced housing that run around each of its four sides.

Entering by the Linden Road entrance with the Portland stone pillars designed by the cemetery's surveyor James Bunstone Bunning, what first strikes the visitor is bird song – woodpeckers, warblers and jays are just three species that make their nests here – and the sounds will accompany you on your visit. Keen lepidopterists may even spot the 16 species of butterfly that have been found here.

Once the visitor has ceased looking upward, the eye is taken along the central lime and linden tree-lined avenue, gently rising to the magnificent facade of the ruined, roofless Anglican chapel (again, that modesty: in the style of Decorated Gothic, this looks more like a small medieval cathedral). There was also once, nearer the entrance, a Nonconformist chapel, but this was demolished more than 40 years ago having suffered wartime bomb damage.

The eye's attraction is immediate but this is an initial distraction from Bunning's two lodges (both, like the chapel, are Grade II listed) that stand like sentinels (even if one is now severely wounded) immediately within the gates. Both were threatened with demolition after they fell into dilapidation, but the West Lodge was restored in the 1980s to a creamy, square, symmetrical, neo-classical building with a porticoed entrance. Remarkably, it is now a private home with no connection with the cemetery. The East Lodge is a sorry sight: there is cracked brick and exposed plaster, the entry steps have fallen in, the roof and windows are open to the elements and are protected only by a corrugated iron canopy mounted on scaffolding. However, the Friends of

Nunhead Cemetery still hope that it may be restored to its former elegance and usefulness.

One may be tempted to begin the visit by walking up that central avenue but this would not be the best or the most productive way to see what Nunhead offers. The cemetery may be 52 acres but it is not difficult to walk most of its paths and see all there is to see in two or so hours if one is armed with a useful map and guide from the Friends' association. The paths loop east and west, north and south and cross toward the centre at various points. There are also much narrower paths that lead to hidden places in the tangled interior that are not marked on the map.

The cemetery's advocates like to stress the Victorian gloom, but also, rightly, that walking its paths is often like a stroll down remote country lanes. One meets the occasional jogger and dog walker, and one passes the oak, holly, horse chestnut, holm oak and ginkgo (or maidenhair) trees that shroud the paths.

However, this impression of bucolic bliss is not quite as it seems. If one turns left at the gates and takes the Catacomb Path or The Loop, both of which lead to the East Path (one could as profitably turn right as I explain below), on either side of these paths, and deep in the woods, are ivy-clad, moss-green headstones. Some are leaning toward a neighbour as if confiding about who lies below and some seem frozen, stricken, about to topple. There are fallen columns, crooked monuments, almost sunken tombs – many are hidden or half-hidden and looked down on by ash and sycamore trees. What covers the dead is often itself covered. An angel, her hands gone, seems to beseech heaven, for the distress of what surrounds her.

There are also open, richly green (if less interesting) areas of the cemetery where there are new burials. This includes a small Muslim area, where many of the headstones are heart shaped and bear the crescent.

Built in 1840 by the London Cemetery Company, after a slow start – there were nine burials in the first six months and 130 in the first year – it prospered with 200 burials a year over the next 25 years. However, after that Nunhead encountered difficulties. The death of its first superintendent revealed an embezzlement of many thousands of pounds; the local burial board threatened a takeover; there was an economic recession; and mortality rates were falling. Yet, Nunhead survived – indeed prospered – and the next half century saw the erection of greenhouses (now long gone) and a new south entrance. However, plans to open a crematorium in 1911 came to nothing. The inter-war rise in maintenance costs and wage bills, the taking of the railings for scrap during the Second World War, along with vandalism – the Anglican chapel was burnt by vandals in 1974 – caused Nunhead to decline. By 1969, the owners, United Cemeteries, went out of business with annual losses of £5,000 and after plans to develop some of the land had fallen foul of local reaction.

There were seven sets of catacombs in Nunhead Cemetery: Eastern Catacombs, four cylindrical catacombs (two of which were never used), and catacombs beneath the Anglican chapel and the Dissenters' chapel. Only the roof of the Eastern Catacomb can be seen today on the Catacomb Path behind the gingko tree. The Anglican chapel catacombs may be viewed on Friends' open days and during their annual Open House weekend.

The catacombs had all been plundered for their lead and jewellery; coffins were opened and bones scattered about. One of the catacombs contains 23 large cases of remains and 12 lead coffins disinterred from the churchyard of what had been the Wren church of St Christopher-le-Stocks, which itself had replaced a 13th century church destroyed in the Great Fire of London. The Wren Church was demolished in 1781 to make way for the rebuilding of the Bank of England. The remainder of the churchyard disappeared in the mid-1860s as the bank further expanded. In the 20th century more burial vaults were cleared as the bank continued to grow and the last remains were interred in Nunhead in 1953. The vaults are marked by two large ledger stones on the Catacomb Path.

While what was man-made often decayed or was looted or broken, the trees and the undergrowth flourished to such an extent that the cemetery was being lost to a wilderness. In 1975, the London Borough of Southwark was able to buy Nunhead for £1 under an Act of Parliament.

However, the council's ambitious £500,000 plans, sanctioned by an Act of Parliament, to create Waverley Park, a 22 acre nature reserve, which would have comprised most of the cemetery and land set aside to allow for another half century of burials, faltered. The cemetery remains open for interments in family plots. The Friends' association was founded in 1981. Together with the council they have worked to save and maintain the cemetery, aided by a Heritage Lottery Fund grant of £1.5 million, which, among other things, paid for the restoration of the West Lodge and the chapel's stabilisation, as well as work on the boundary railings and the restoration of 50 monuments.

The effort has been publicly recognised: the cemetery has a Grade II* listing; it is a designated Conservation Area, a Site of Metropolitan Importance for Wildlife and a local nature reserve. In addition to the West Lodge and the chapel, 10 monuments are Grade II listed.

Unlike some of the other of the Magnificent Seven, Nunhead is not notable for the famous who have found a final home here. There are many distinguished people buried here but most are now not publicly known. The first burial was Charles Abbott, a 101-year-old Ipswich grocer and a brother (or resident) at the Charterhouse almshouse (see Tower Hamlets Cemetery, page 124). He was joined by, among many others, Frederick Beckwith (1821–1898), who achieved the remarkable feat of being the world swimming champion when 'really only a passable swimmer', and his son William (1857–1892). He was also a champion swimmer who began competitive swimming at five under the name of 'Baby Beckwith, the Wonder of the World'. There was also William 'Mutton' Davies (1795–1867). He was a boxer, wrestler and acrobat who gained his nickname from his preferred dish that was always ordered at dinner. Other companions in death are Field Marshal Sir William Gomm (1784–1875), who joined the army at 10 and went on to fight in the Peninsular campaign and at Waterloo, and became commander-in-chief in India; and Harriet Tebbutt (1815–1893). She was a nurse who was the superintendent of the Scutari Hospital under Florence Nightingale in the Crimea.

There are also several luminaries of the music hall to be found here, like the singer Jenny Hill (1841–1896) and Augustus Durandeau (1848–1893), who wrote 'It's a Long Way to Tipperary' and other popular songs. Hers is a difficult grave to find, while his resting place in a common grave is now marked. Edward Weston owned the Six Cans and Punchbowl pub in High Holborn and converted a disused chapel behind it for entertainment as Weston's Music Hall. He sold it and the site became the Holborn Empire where Albert Chevalier (see Abney Park, page 18), Ada Reeves, Dan Leno and Gracie Fields performed.

There are two small sections for war graves maintained by the Commonwealth War Graves Commission. The first, from the First World War, surprises one by its whiteness set against the green of the woodland paths. Here lie soldiers from Canada, South Africa, and New Zealand together with one Australian. Slightly further on are Australian soldiers' graves, surrounded by a well-kept hedge.

Next to the First World War graves is the plot where nine local boys are buried. They were aged 11 to 14 and died in a boating accident in the Thames in 1912. Until it was stolen in 1969, there was here a life-sized bronze figure of a scout, his head bowed on Sir Giles Gilbert Scott's cenotaph. The local council, aided by the Friends, have placed a beautiful white marble open book on the spot, where the names of the boys are inscribed.

The most impressive of Nunhead's tombs – in a cemetery where, it has to be said, there is not much competition – is the sarcophagus of John Allan

(1790–1865) and his family, set on a cracked, ugly brick plinth. His bas-relief portrait is set in the rear. The tomb is based on that of Payava of Xanthos. For one who rests in so grand a place, all we seem to know of Allan is that he was a Yorkshireman who made his money in shipping.

Just along the path from the Allan tomb is the cemetery's only surviving mausoleum: that of the Stearne family built in about 1900 and now restored. (In the years of the cemetery's decline, vandals entered it.) It is of brick and faced with terracotta tiles with a Romanesque-like decoration around its entrance. We know even less of Mr Stearnes and his family than we do of their neighbours, the Allans.

By contrast, the humble grave of George Howell (1833–1910) is not easy to find down the quiet Lower Cross Path. George left school at eight and became a Lib-Lab MP for Bethnal Green and first general secretary of the TUC.

If one has taken the East path, then it is at the very end that one comes to the most striking construction, apart from the chapel: the obelisk dedicated to the 'Scottish Martyrs'. Not that it can be missed on entry as it is 50 feet away to the right after entering the main gates. This commemorates the trials in Edinburgh of five men – Thomas Muir, Thomas Fyshe Palmer, William Skirving, Maurice Margorot and Joseph Gerald – which led them to be transported to Australia in 1794 and 1795 for advocating parliamentary reform. The Grade II listed, 33-feet high, five-sided granite obelisk, which weighs 40 tonnes, was paid for by a collection at a public meeting in London in 1837. Erected in 1851, the initiative came from Joseph Hume, the radical Scottish MP who was responsible for the martyrs' other memorial raised in Edinburgh. The belief is that Nunhead was chosen due to the plethora of coffee houses – which were hotbeds of radical thought – in nearby Southwark at that time.

The obelisk can be reached after walking down the hill away from the view of St Paul's, and before that to the right is the Wetland area, where volunteers have created a pond. Also near here is the Schroeter and Oppenheim family vault with its bas-relief sculptures, which, sadly, is not in a good state of repair.

Between here and the obelisk is also the monument to the wonderfully named Sir Polydor de Keyser (1832–1898). He was the Belgium-born hotel proprietor who was the first Catholic to be elected Lord Mayor of London since the Reformation less than 300 years before. He attained his municipal eminence when the Emancipation Act (1829) ended the bar on Catholics holding public office.

At the other end of the Christian spectrum comes the Dissenters' Row. The Dissenters' chapel once stood here. On unconsecrated ground are a mixture of Celtic crosses, crosses, columns and obelisks commemorating notable Baptists, Methodists and Congregationalists. One of these was the Rev John Wells (died 1872). He was a self-educated Baptist minister who was raised in the workhouse and would preach to 2,000 people at his tabernacle in Wansey Street, Wandsworth. An inscription tells us that the monument was raised by his 'sorrowing' church and congregation.

If, instead of taking the East Path at the beginning of the walk, the visitor has turned right at the gate and gone past the Martyrs' memorial and walked up West Hill, this would have led to Nunhead's highest point. The obelisk of the Victorian engineer William Chadwick (1797–1852), which was pulled up a steep incline of the hill by men and horses to reach the spot, stands here. Turn from here and one is greeted with a magnificent sight. Through a window of trees, created in 2000/2001 with some of the Heritage Lottery Fund grant, lies St Paul's Cathedral 200 feet below and the City of London lies five miles to the north. It is as if the cemetery and its inhabitants are keeping watch on the city below.

Getting there
Nunhead rail station

Friends' association
Yes

Tours
Yes

Take a break
Manze's Eel and Pie House, 156 Peckham High Street SE15

Something else to see
55 Underhill Road SE22, former home of the novelist CS Forester, marked by a blue plaque.

Old St Pancras Churchyard

Pancras Road NW1

The small, High Anglican Old St Pancras Church is all too used to the incursions of the railway. It sits on a hill off the busy road below, minutes from three of the main London terminals – St Pancras, King's Cross and Euston. In the 1860s, the churchyard was first encroached on when the Midland railway was cut through, while the work on the new St Pancras International Station also caused incursions to the extent that remains were exhumed and reburied in 2003 in Finchley (St Pancras and Islington) Cemetery (see page 56).

In *Dombey and Son*, Charles Dickens recorded a 'great earthquake' that rent the whole neighbourhood when the railway cut through the area that was his childhood home. There is a poignant reminder of that Victorian construction in the churchyard today. The Hardy Tree stands behind the church that marks where the unidentified fragments of those disinterred from the graves to make way for Victorian modern travel were placed in a deep pit by an unfortunate young architect, who was to forsake this first profession for that of novelist. Thomas Hardy was charged by the architect Sir Arthur Blomfield to dismantle the tombs and disinter the remains. Now the ash tree has flourished and around its broad trunk are the headstones that were placed there 150 years ago beneath its foliage cluster, like beseeching children.

In his poem 'The Levelled Churchyard', Hardy wrote:

'O Passenger, pray list and catch
Our signs and piteous groans,
Half stifled in this jumbled patch
Of wrenched memorial stones!

We late-lamented, resting here
Are mixed to human jam,
And each to each exclaims in fear,
"I know not which I am!"'

Old St Pancras Churchyard has not gone wholly the way of most London churchyards: turned into public gardens where all that remains of their former selves are gravestones wedged up against a perimeter wall. True, the churchyard is classified as a garden – and a very pleasant one it is, covered in autumn leaves when I visited one November day, after having passed through the beautiful decorated iron gates at the entrance – but there are more than enough interesting graves and memorials to warrant a visitor's time. It has

a hilly aspect and there is a general atmosphere of surprising quietness and calm in the middle of a busy area in one of the world's busiest cities.

The church is, in fact, one of the oldest places of worship in the country. Drastically restored and enlarged in 1848, this meant, among other things, that the west tower was destroyed. There has been a church here since 314 AD. According to one antiquarian authority, the hill on which the church stands (which most definitely was, at one time, a Roman encampment) was the site of a pagan compitium or rural shrine, which was converted to Christian use even before St Augustine's mission. Part of the internal north wall has exposed Norman masonry.

The churchyard was closed for burials in 1854 and the gardens were opened in 1877. There are actually two churchyards on the one site – those of Old St Pancras and the extension of St Giles-in-the-Fields (see And elsewhere..., page 144) as the two churches were once part of one parish.

As well as Hardy's tree, another reminder of those whose graves can no longer be seen is the large Gothic memorial, which is surmounted by a spire that contains a sundial and reliefs of St Giles and St Pancras. The whole structure is guarded by four stone dog-like creatures and is made of Portland stone, marble, granite and red Mansfield stone, with mosaic enrichment. This was presented by the philanthropist and social reformer Baroness Burdett-Coutts, when the local authority laid out the gardens and undertook the task of moving the headstones and levelling the ground. Each of its panel contains

a long list of often very unusual but distinguished names – aristocrats and a Turkish ambassador among them – and the inscription reminds us that 'those who were severed by lineage, race, faith, clime' have been gathered together on this spot.

This monument is only challenged by that of Sir John Soane and his wife (she died in 1815; he joined her in 1837). He was an architect and creator of the London museum and house where he once lived. The museum was established, after his death, by an Act of Parliament that he had negotiated.

Under a plain stone rests 'the English Bach' or 'the London Bach', Johann Christian (1735–1782), son of Johann Sebastian, on the north side of the Burdett-Coutts obelisk.

One unusual fact about this churchyard is that so many people from overseas, many of whom presumably did not share the Anglican or even Protestant faith, are buried here. For example, when the churchyard was dug up, the remains of distinguished French Roman Catholic *émigrés*, who lived in nearby Somers Town, were returned to their native land for burial. The bones of Filippo Antonio Pasquali de Paoli, 'The Patriot', framer of Corsica's first democratic constitution and its first president, were repatriated to that island in 1889. His bust is in Westminster Abbey.

There is an earlier literary connection than Hardy's. When the area was 'one mile from London', the poet Percy Bysse Shelley, lodging nearby, saw and fell in love with Mary Godwin (later to write *Frankenstein*). She was visiting the grave of her mother Mary Wollstonecraft (1759–1797), who wrote *Vindication of the Rights of Women*. He left his pregnant first wife and eloped with Mary in 1814. Mary senior's husband, the philosopher William Godwin (1756–1836) was also buried here as they lived a short distance away, but their bodies were moved to the churchyard of St Peter's, Bournemouth. Today they rest there in a large square tomb, with their daughter and Shelley's heart. (The Old St Pancras guide makes the common error of not referring to the exhumation and reburial when directing one to the large tomb that once held them.)

The family grave of the Rhodes family was restored by the businessman and imperialist Cecil Rhodes himself in 1890. (Visitors will have to travel further afield to visit his final resting place, though. He lies on a hilltop in Zimbabwe.)

The origins of the diverse population of the area (Somalis and other asylum seekers have followed the Greek Cypriots, who themselves followed the Irish who first came as builders of the railway) is evidenced by the stones in a sheltered corner of the bottom of the churchyard that display French names. They fled toward the end of the 18th century from the Terror that followed the French revolution and settled in the area. In 2006, during work on the new St Pancras International Station, the grave of the French archbishop Arthur Richard Dillon was found, and among the remains were his porcelain false teeth. Dillon had been a member of the Assembly of Notables convened by King Louis XVI. He had also lived in great wealth, keeping an extravagant hunt, in a chateau with his wealthy, widowed niece. It was assumed that they were lovers. In 2007 his remains went to Narbonne Cathedral and his teeth went to the Museum of London.

Getting there
Kings Cross and St Pancras tube station

Friends' association
No

Tours
No

Take a break
Restaurant (or café), The British Library, Euston Road NW1

Something else to see
The British Library, Euston Road NW1

St John at Hampstead Old Churchyard and Additional Burial Ground

Church Row NW3

Hampstead is the most charming – and the most expensive – of London's urban villages. It is settled on a hill, with winding, narrow, hilly lanes and streets. There are pretty houses, cottages and sumptuous mansions, a variety of small shops, and many interesting places to visit. If its crown is the Heath, then one of its hidden gems is surely St John's Church and its two burial grounds. These sit at the end of Church Row, which is an elegant 18th century terrace that takes one to the gates of the Old Churchyard and surrounds the church. The gates and railings came from Cannons, the demolished home of the Duke of Chandos near Edgware.

There are few, if any, churchyards in London (or, for that matter, in any city) so well preserved and very much as our great-grandparents might have seen them: no graves have been cleared to create a garden; no headstones have been pushed up against surrounding walls; no decaying table tombs have been encased in concrete. But there are also very few (if any) city burial places – not even Bunhill Fields (see page 36) – with such a collection of illustrious dead and a variety of monuments. Indeed, St John's rivals the great Victorian cemeteries in proportion to its size.

There may have been some kind of religious building here after the granting of a charter to the Benedictines of Westminster Abbey in 986. However, the first references to a church do not occur until 1312 and parish records run continuously from 1540.

By 1744, the church – part stone, part timber and with a small wooden tower – was becoming so dangerous as to deter worshippers. The church underwent a radical reconstruction and was reconsecrated in 1747. It was extended and improved again in the next century, with additions made in 1911–1912 and again in 1964 and 1989. A redecoration of the church in 1958 swept away the dark Victorian interior and restored the lightness of the original church of 1747. There are several notable memorials in the church, including a bust of John Keats who lived nearby, but who rests in the Protestant Cemetery in Rome under a small pyramid that does not name him and refers only to 'a young English poet' and 'One Whose Name was writ in water'.

The wish by the trustees to move the tower led to a long-running controversy. It was won in part by the efforts of some of those who now rest beneath its shadow in the Old Churchyard. Among the members of the Committee for the Preservation of the Tower was Sir Sidney Colvin (1845–1927). He was Keats' biographer and a friend of Robert Louis Stevenson, with whom he lodged nearby. Another was Richard Norman Shaw (1831–1912), who rests with his wife and both parents in a finely decorated chest tomb, which is most suitable for the man who was champion of the Queen Anne Revival in architecture. The tall chimneys of the house he designed for himself at 6 Ellerdale Road can be viewed to the south east.

Fellow architect George Gilbert Scott Junior (1839–1897) joined Shaw on the committee. He rests in the church's second cemetery, the Additional Burial Ground, across the lane. He was the restorer of several Oxbridge colleges, and son of the architect Sir Gilbert and father of Sir Giles. Also buried here is his youngest son, Adrian (1882–1963), who designed his own house in the village and was responsible for the Lansbury Estate in east London.

There has been a very deliberate (and successful) policy to create a refuge for many different species of plants, trees, birds, and animals (Camden Council is responsible for the upkeep of the grounds) in both churchyards. There are cedar of Lebanon, beech and oak trees. Nuthatch, long-tailed tits, wrens and jays nest here, and bats also find a home here. There are different kinds of grasses and wildflowers, like white clover, creeping buttercup and agrimony, among which one finds butterflies like the gatekeeper and speckled wood. The vegetated walls and tombstones encourage male fern, hart's tongue and numerous species of mosses and lichens.

Both burial places are set on slight slopes – in the Old Churchyard, the ground falls away to the south and west of the church – and both sites are very easy to walk in. There is no problem in stepping between graves in the churchyard and the Additional Burial Ground has wide paths from top to bottom, with paths running across.

Two very helpful 'tomb trails' are provided, for a church donation (though, it has to be said, that the map for the Additional Burial Ground is far less easy to understand than the fixed one provided at the entrance gate).

It would be easy to miss the pathetic grave of Henry Cort (1740–1800) when coming through the gates into the Old Churchyard. It is near the entrance and not easy to find as Thomas Gardnor's imposing pedestal tomb with urn and railings looms over it. Cort's inscription is not easy to read, but we are told 'He died a broken-hearted man' after his daughter had predeceased him and his business failed (he patented the process of purifying iron) when his partner embezzled the company.

The Old Churchyard's most famous resident is the painter John Constable (1776–1837), born in Suffolk, and a Hampstead resident until three years before his death. His railinged, Grade II listed chest tomb is one of the furthest from the church, on a shady path in the south east corner. Constable is joined further along this path by William Purton (died 1843), who was one of his closest friends in the village.

There are two pointers to graves by the church. One is to that of Constable and the other to the Grade II listed chest tomb of John Harrison (1693–1776), by the side of the church's north wall. He invented the marine chronometer and so 'discovered' longitude. The tomb was paid for by the Worshipful Company of Clockmakers. One panel describes the invention and Harrison's struggle to obtain the Longitude Prize. Another tells of his son, William (1728–1815) who is also buried here with his mother Elizabeth (died 1777) and two brothers. He is described as custodian of the watch to Jamaica and Barbados for the trials at sea.

Not far away is Joanna Baillie (1762–1851) who rests in a chest tomb with railings that were only restored in 2010. She was one of the most famous women dramatists of her day and also the niece of William and John Hunter, the surgeons and anatomists.

Given that they were contemporaries, one wonders if she ever met Philadelphia Hancock (1730–1792) and her daughter Elizabeth Austen (1761–1931), who are also buried here. Though I do not know if they lived in the village at the same time, it is nice to reflect that Philadelphia and Elizabeth could have talked to Joanna about their niece and cousin, who had literary ambitions. She was Jane Austen; Elizabeth later became Jane's sister-in-law when she married Jane's brother, Henry.

The Additional Burial Ground was laid out in 1812 when the Old Churchyard became overcrowded. While it is closed for burials, it remains open for the interment of cremated remains.

In 1940, in the northeast corner of this section a delightful wooden cloister reflecting Arts and Crafts influence was added as a space for memorial tablets (there is also at the other end of the path a memorial garden for the same purpose). In the cloister one notices a large number of plaques to members of the Soskice family, relatives of Sir Frank Soskice (1902–1997). He was a one-time Labour attorney-general, solicitor-general and home secretary, whose grave is only a few yards away. (His grandfather, the novelist Ford Maddox Ford, was one of those who battled to save the tower.) Soskice is buried next to EV Knox (1881–1971), the editor of *Punch,* whose niece, the novelist Penelope Fitzgerald (1916–2000), has a tablet of green slate on the grave. (Knox was a pew owner and the brass plate bearing his name is the only one still attached to a pew.)

A colleague of Soskice, Hugh Gaitskell (1906–1963), leader of the Labour Party, finds himself in an interesting gathering in the southeast corner. Gaitskell is buried with his wife, Dora (1901–1989), a life peer. His is unusual for a contemporary memorial – and unusual, too, perhaps for a Labour leader: it is a large urn that sits on a substantial podium in Portland stone. At right angles to him is the lovely headstone of Kay Kendall (1927–1959) in green slate, with splendid script and whirls. She is the actress and third wife of the actor Rex Harrison, who went on to marry three more wives.

Next to Gaitskell is the oldest wooden deadboard in the cemetery (I could only find one other but there may be more) placed to mark the resting place of George Busson du Maurier (1834–1869), the *Punch* cartoonist and author of *Trilby.* Among other family members buried with him is his son Sir Gerald (1873–1934), the actor-manager who was the father of Daphne du Maurier, the novelist. However, Gerald and the other family members' presence are not easy to see as they are listed on metal plaques in miniscule script. (Daphne is not here: she was cremated and her ashes scattered near her Cornish home.)

Across from the Du Mauriers' grave is the fine headstone with relief lettering which marks the resting place of Sylvia (1866–1910), George du Maurier's daughter, and her husband Arthur Llewelyn Davies (1863–1907). With their early deaths their five sons were unofficially adopted by JM Barrie, who was already inspired by the story of the 'lost boys', to write *Peter Pan.*

This comparatively small burial ground has other literary associations. Lady Anne Isabella Thackeray Ritchie (1837–1919) was the eldest daughter of William Makepeace Thackeray, the novelist, and aunt of Virginia Woolf. Lady Anne was herself a novelist and biographer of her father and his friends. Arthur Waugh (1866–1943) was a publisher with Chapman & Hall and father of the novelists Evelyn and Alec. (The latter's ashes are interred in the grave.) AR Orage (1873–1934), a radical journalist, lies beneath a large, flat, slate ledger stone with lettering thought to be by Eric Gill. It is topped by a curious circular device that has been described as being 'a circle, divided by crisscross lines until it looked like a fly's eye'.

Mary Frances Hammersley's Grade II listed tomb is the most striking of the few that are in the Additional Burial Ground. It is a tall shrine – made of limestone

– on a pedestal, with a bronze statue of a winged youth holding a sleeping girl. The collective memorial that should not be missed is the 'Soldiers' daughters – Second vault'. This is a common grave and an extension of the 1812 grave for girls from local 'homes', that is, orphanages. They would have lived locally in the now no longer extant Royal Soldiers' Daughters' Home and trained for domestic service. This was started after the Crimea War. The name of each girl, listed on the panels of either side of the attractive horizontal monument, appears with her dates and her father's regiment. A few are in their early 20s, most in their teens or younger, and one only a year old.

Far from home rests Eva Gore-Booth (1870–1926) under a tall headstone of yellow sandstone. This is ironic as she was not only a poet, suffragette, and friend of the poet WB Yeats, but also an Irish nationalist.

Amid the scholarship, politics, literature and architecture, St John's also offers a London tradition. There is a spot where the poet Eleanor Farjeon (1881–1965) and the philosopher and broadcaster CM Joad (1881–1953) lie near each other. Under a white marble headstone, almost next to them, rest Bert Matthews (1884–1970) and his wife Rebecca (1884–1963), the pearly king and queen of Camden. A tablet also commemorates their daughter Rose Matthews Smith and son-in-law George Smith (died 1986), who 'carried on this charitable tradition'. Bert also had another unusual calling: for 40 years he was Hampstead's official rat catcher.

Getting there
Hampstead tube station

Friends' association
No

Tours
No

Take a break
The Horseshoe, 28 Heath Street NW3

Something else to see
Keats' House, Keats' Grove NW3

St Mary's Roman Catholic Cemetery

Harrow Road NW10

granite stone. This is the Jesuit memorial but, alas, the names are mostly indecipherable.

In a more popular branch of entertainment, someone much better known than even Barbirolli in his day but now unlikely to be known by anyone under 60 is Gilbert Harding (1907-1960). Famously grumpy, even rude, the bow-tied television panellist was a convert to Catholicism largely under the influence of GK Chesterton. In a famous *Face to Face* interview with John Freeman, he said: 'I should much rather be dead than alive, if I hadn't got to go through the miseries of actually dying'. Eight weeks later he collapsed and died on the steps of Broadcasting House. He lies beneath a simple, flat, stepped stone between the two mausoleums nearest the Belgian memorial.

Appropriately, the 'poet of Catholicism', Francis Thompson (1859–1907) rests here, in a large, plain table tomb, with an inscription lettered by Eric Gill, his hound of heaven having no doubt caught up with him after that long poetic pursuit 'down the nights and down the days ... down the arches of the years ... down the labyrinthine ways'.

Another Catholic poet in these grounds is Alice Meynell (1847–1922). She was a close friend and editor of Thompson and supported him when he was recovering from opium addiction. She was herself considered for the poet laureateship when Tennyson died. Her weathered flat stone, like a tablet on a base, bears only her name and date of death. A writer of a different stripe, who also rests here in a family grave with his parents and his wife, is Arthur Henry Furey (1883–1959), better known as Sax Rohmer, the creator of Fu Manchu.

TP (Thomas Power) O'Connor (1848–1929) is buried beneath what looks like a war memorial – a column surmounted by a cross at the foot of which is a plinth. The words engraved tell us that he was an 'orator-statesman-journalist-Irish patriot-tribune of the people', as well as a 'citizen of the world'.

Sir James Melville (1885–1931), another MP, is buried in front of O'Connor's memorial. On his election in 1929, Melville was appointed solicitor-general in the second Labour government but resigned a year later. The next year, the government fell and he died.

Another Irish-born MP, Irish nationalist and journalist in St Mary's is Hugh Delargy (1908–1976), at one time Labour MP for Thurrock. His badly weathered stone (opposite the toilets) marks the interment of his ashes, and pays tribute to him both as an MP and also as Knight Commander Grand Cross Polonia Restituta, one of the highest orders to be awarded by the then Polish government in exile.

There cannot be many cemeteries where three spies are interred, but one is St Mary's. Lying in an unmarked grave is Josef Jakobs (1898–1941), a German corporal parachuted into Huntingdonshire, England. He was apprehended, court marshalled for treachery, and died before a firing squad. He was the last person executed in the Tower of London.

Elsewhere is Krystyna Skarbek (1915–1952), who was born in Poland. She joined the British Secret Intelligence where she took the *nom de guerre* Christine Granville, which she adopted by deed poll after the war. In her operations she worked with Andrzej Kowerski (1912–1988), a special operations executive agent in the Second World War, who used the assumed name Andrew Kennedy. At one time they were captured by the Gestapo. She was murdered in a London hotel, where she was staying, when planning to join him abroad the next day, having been unsuccessful in her post-war jobs. Upon his death, his ashes were interred in her grave.

Their grave has a shield on the headstone with her details and a tablet at the base containing his. On top of her headstone is a tall cross, at the junction of which is a shield depicting the White Eagle of Poland and the Black Virgin of Czestochowa.

Like the two Jewish cemeteries at Willesden (see page 132), St Mary's has its story to tell of those who came to these shores and died here. There are the aristocratic and rich Catholics, but there are also the less distinguished and poor, Poles, Irish and Italians. They came to seek a better life, often at times when being Catholic added to life's burdens.

Getting there
Kensal Green tube station

Friends' association
No

Tours
No

Take a break
The Mason's Arms, Harrow Road NW10

Something else to see
Queen's Park Farmer's Market, Salusbury Road Primary School NW6 (Sundays 10am to 2pm only)

Tower Hamlets Cemetery

Southern Grove E3

Tower Hamlets Cemetery stands in the middle of one of the poorest areas in the UK. Its present state may appear to attest to that fact. Despite the heroic conservation and maintenance work of the Friends' association that was founded in 1990, the place has a slightly neglected air. It is the poor relation, the forgotten cousin in the family of the Magnificent Seven. There are broad paths and many graves are easy to see, but many others are obscured, half or completely hidden by ivy or in thick clusters of undergrowth. Some stones are severely weathered, their inscriptions indecipherable; many are broken or have toppled or sunk.

However, restoration has ensured that sensitive tree and vegetation clearance has opened up some areas, which allows more graves to be seen. Whatever its problems, Tower Hamlets is an interesting cemetery with a long history and some remarkable graves. It does, though, lack the atmosphere to be found at, say, Highgate, Nunhead or even West Norwood. This may be partly due to the fact that one does not have the feeling of being enclosed, even cut off from the world as one feels once through the gates of these other cemeteries. Its high brick walls may be on the National Register of listed buildings, but they do not surround it completely. Railings allow visitors to look out to the surrounding streets while brash, modern blocks of flats look in.

In 1952, Sir Nicholas Pevsner referred to the cemetery as 'astonishingly overcrowded and overgrown'. Some of the state of the cemetery is undoubtedly due to the years when it was closed and unguarded. It became the target of vandals and was used as a rubbish dump.

However, the worst vandalism was undertaken after 1966, when the newly born but now long-defunct Greater London Council bought the cemetery and closed it for burials. The Council decided to clear almost all of the graves to create a park. Apart from anything else, this was an act of extraordinary insensitivity: the cemetery had only been open for 120 years, which meant that the recent and not very distant ancestors of many local residents rested there. The local people who chose to tip rubbish there or desecrate the graves could hardly be said to have much regard for their neighbours' feelings either. Luckily, the GLC was stopped in 1967 after local protests and funding problems, but not before £127,000 had been spent and 0.7 acres of the historic 27 acres of the cemetery had been cleared. The whole site is now a designated Local Nature Reserve and Site of Metropolitan Importance for Nature Conservation. This includes the cemetery and an additional six acres called Scrapyard Meadows and Ackroyd Drive Greenlink, which are both situated at its southern boundary and were added in the mid 1990s. In

2002, the Friends and other local volunteers created the Cantrell Road Maze. Parts of the park are managed wilderness, while others, particularly the two pond areas, are used for teaching environmental science (school parties are frequent visitors). The nature reserve is the borough's first in what is a densely built-up area.

Today, the signs within the railings refer to it as 'a cemetery park' and despite the GLC's depredations, this pocket of nature delights in this poor and overcrowded borough and does not get enough credit. The whole area is designated as a Metropolitan Open Land and Conservation Area, with an outstanding variety of wild plants, flowers and animals (two foxes crossed my path), plus there are 20 species of butterfly and about 35 of birds. The Friends organise not only general tours of the cemetery but there are specialised tours to search for graves, to spot bats, and to 'nibble your way around the park' (a wild food walk), as well as a 'moth morning', and the annual International Dawn Chorus Day walk when the birds are heard to come into their own.

Had the GLC's plans gone ahead, one would see a very large park (no doubt some housing would have been built and a playground and perhaps other amusements erected) and the only graves would have been those along the right hand path behind the green railings that one sees as one enters today. As it is, there are a few large grassy areas amid the existing graves, some bumpy as if the grass has been grown over earth that has not flattened. In the middle of one of these spaces stands the large, granite obelisk that commemorates Charles Francis (died aged 74 in 1861), his wife Ann (died aged 59 in 1876) and daughter Mary. He was a corn merchant and one of the founders of the cemetery. A missing brick on the east side of the monument allows the rising sun to shine through the holes in the wrought iron cross built into the west side.

What this act of municipal vandalism meant in terms of what has been lost can only now be guessed at, but we do know that among the more simple headstones many monuments and memorials were destroyed. In which case, perhaps remarkably, seven graves were listed as Grade II in the year 2000.

The Anglican and Dissenting chapels (the latter, unusually, in a Byzantine style) have been demolished, standing derelict more than 20 years after suffering damage from wartime bombing from which the whole area, so close to London's Docklands, suffered so grievously. (The cemetery was hit five times and shrapnel damage can still be seen on some graves near the Soanes Centre by the entrance. The centre serves as both the Friends' headquarters and also as a place for ecological and environmental courses.)

A lodge and a mortuary in the Egyptian style met the same fate. Their positions are unmarked, but we know that the Anglican chapel stood on what is now a large earthen area, underneath which lie the catacombs (but, again, with no marker). Nearby is the site of the former war memorial. This was in the traditional style of a tall, white, Blomfield 'Cross of Sacrifice' on a stepped base. It was moved due to vandalism and recreated near the entrance as a broad grey and black granite structure, with 16 panels listing the names commemorated.

Originally called The City of London and Tower Hamlets Cemetery, it was opened in 1841 by a company of the same name. It comprised 11 wealthy directors whose occupations included those of corn merchant, merchant ship broker and ship owner and timber merchant. John Pirie was also a director – he was a ship owner and Lord Mayor of London in the year that the cemetery came into being.

However, Mile End – it did not become part of the London Metropolitan area until 1855 – was then, as now, a poor area. While these wealthy businessmen were attracted to it as a new form of enterprise, as was the case with the other Victorian cemeteries, the earliest interments were in pauper (or public) graves.

There were more than 500 burials recorded in 1845 and in 1850 the number was twice as many. By 1889, about 250,000 had found their last resting place here. This was the most working class of London's Victorian cemeteries and in its first two years saw 60% of burials in public graves, and within a decade (1851) the figure was 80%.

Today, one can see the area of the public graves but the multiplicity of headstones is misleading: they mean only that the family of one of the people buried in a grave has been commemorated. Such indignity is shocking. However, perhaps most poignant of all is the fact that 26 of the 172 people (including 62 children), who were crushed to death in the Bethnal Green tube station disaster in 1943, are buried here. The victims were sheltering in the tube station when it was struck by a bomb. All but one of them are buried in public graves (not in the same grave but in the same area) situated behind where the chapel once stood. Most have a small 'public' headstone on which the date is recorded, without mentioning the tragedy.

While some of the local people who died as a result of enemy air raids may be in common graves, they are remembered on the other side of the cemetery by a memorial erected in 1952 and made from bricks taken from bombed properties.

However, not all of those laid to rest in the early years were local people: many sailors who came to the area through its shipping associations are also found here (as are many who were connected with shipping, like engineers, mast makers, and rope makers). Few, though, met such an unfortunate death as Captain Lusby, who was accidentally shot in 1874 on his boat when it was moored in London. Peter York Slader also met with an unfortunate death. He was only 14 in 1848 when he drowned after falling off the masthead of a ship at West India Dock.

The worst tragedy of all, though, was the loss of more than 600 people in 1871, when 'Princess Alice', a wooden pleasure steamer returning from Southend collided with an 891-tonne screw iron collier called 'Bywell Castle'. Twenty-eight of the victims lie here, nine in private graves and the rest in public graves, the location of which are unknown.

One of the victims was John Northey, a local headmaster, who it is thought took the trip while his school was having an outing closer to home. His inscription refers to 'one whose loss they [his school and family] so greatly mourn'. Other passengers on the 'Princess Alice' buried in the cemetery are Sarah Ann Forsdike and her three children, and William Alfred Fisher.

Other victims from another loss at sea who are buried at Tower Hamlets are Henry Mead, aged 31, and 22 year-old James Mead, related to one another and watermen. They were killed following a collision with the Woolwich steam packet, 'Plover'.

Three policemen from Leman Street Police Station, Limehouse, are buried in one grave, although they died over a period of six years. PC Richard Barber died in 1884 when chasing a suspect across a railway roof and falling through a skylight; PC William Pasher drowned on holiday in Margate; and PC Ernest Thompson was killed in 1900 when he was stabbed in the neck in Union Street.

One of the most attractively renovated graves is that of the trade unionist and MP Will Crooks (1852–1921), whose large, rough granite stone has a marble memorial, with surrounding rolls, set into it. It tells us: 'He lived and died a servant of the people'. He served on Poplar Council, the London County Council and as an MP for Woolwich. He spoke at mass meetings to raise funds for the great dockworkers' strike of 1889. Crooks is the most publicly notable of the cemetery's residents.

A man Crooks would have known and who was one of the leaders of that strike lies next to him under a small, less well maintained stone. This is Harry Orbell (1858–1914), an organiser of the Dock, Wharf, Riverside and General Workers Union, which provided the money for his memorial, and a founder of the Independent Labour Party.

Both Crooks and Orbell would very likely have attended the funeral in 1887 of Alfred Linnell, who died as a result of a police charge in Trafalgar Square when he took part in Bloody Sunday, a trade union and socialist demonstration. His funeral procession, which began six miles away in Soho, saw thousands lining the route. However, as the coffin came to the cemetery, most mourners had been deterred by dusk and rain and the final interment was attended by comparatively few. Those who stayed heard the 'hymn' to their fallen comrade, chanted by its composer William Morris, the writer and socialist pioneer.

What Tower Hamlets lacks in the graves of the famous it makes up for in lists of the unusual, eccentric and others whose contributions are less well known or forgotten. Not far from the graves of Crooks and Orbell is that of the Rev David Roe, a Wesleyan Methodist minister (died aged 74 in 1921), his wife, Annie Marie and their son Clarence. A rather different kind of public benefactor was Mrs Clara Grant (1868–1950) known as the 'the farthing bundle woman of Bow'. She was a local headteacher, who would give to local poor children bundles of small gifts donated by her friends. She founded the Fern Street Settlement, which brought health visiting to local homes. A library was also opened, along with educational classes being provided, and the Settlement continues today.

Of the unusual people here are the Jamrach family, who imported exotic animals for zoos and circuses. Along from them lies Charles (Charlie) Brown (1893–1932). He was a famous publican of the nearby Railway Tavern whose funeral attracted 10,000 people. Sadly, his red granite stone lies broken (though the inscription is clear) at the foot of the tall monument of a Celtic cross, with an angel for his wife and son. His father, also called Charles, lies next to them.

Two people of military distinction are Captain John Buckley (1813–1876), who won a VC at the Indian Mutiny (his two wives and eight children either died of disease or were murdered in India) and Thomas Mullins (1839–1899), who took part in the Charge of the Light Brigade at the Battle of Balaclava. Another interred here is Hannah Maria Purcell (died 1843), renowned as the widowed second wife of William Purcell, who was one of the last survivors of the Mutiny on the Bounty. The inscription refers to the crew's 'forty-five days in their boat in the Pacific Ocean ... and having travelled three thousand six hundred miles they landed at Timor where they were most hospitably received by the Dutch Governor'.

There are also painted headstones, set in rows, to mark the graves of former residents of Sutton's Hospital of the Charterhouse in Clerkenwell, founded in 1614. They rest six to a grave. Charterhouse still exists today and its residents (all men) are still called 'brothers'.

Despite the Grade II listings, there is only one memorial that is striking: a corner plot for the listed, spire-topped, 30-foot memorial (rather like a smaller, less elaborate stone version of the Albert Memorial) to Joseph Westwood (died 1883), an iron ship builder. His works football team became what is now West Ham United or 'The Hammers'.

Next to the large flat stone to the right of Westwood's memorial is a bare, small piece of earth. With no stone and no inscription, Dr Thomas Barnardo laid to rest three of his own children. Less than a mile away he established his first home for abandoned and neglected children.

Getting there
Mile End tube station

Friends' association
Yes

Tours
Yes

Take a break
E Pellicci, 332 Bethnal Green Road E2

Something else to see
A walk along the towpath of the Grand Union Canal

United Synagogue Cemetery

Beaconsfield Road NW10

Liberal Synagogue Cemetery

Pound Lane NW10

When Mark Twain stayed at the now demolished Dollis Hill House in 1900, he that said Dollis Hill was 'as near to paradise' as any home he knew. Times have changed. One leaves the station to pass along a very nondescript early 20th century, uniform and dull residential street, typical of the area and well littered. The area consists of small shops, whose businesses are not always easy to work out, a large bus station, cheap eating places, the inevitable superstore, and a heavy-looking magistrates' court.

Even the large United Synagogue Cemetery (Beaconsfield Road), with so many distinguished residents and one of the very few reasons for visiting the area, is not easy to find. Crossing the High Road one walks through what appears at first to be a car repair plant (warning: this is plainly marked 'No through road' even though it is one) but is, one finds, a ramshackle little industrial estate. One emerges at the other end to find Beaconsfield Road to the right across the street. There is a large green gate to the cemetery, where a ring on the bell gains entry.

This is a sacred place first and foremost, not a nature reserve or haunt for the curious or historians. Men and women visitors should wear something to cover their heads (available at the cemetery office if someone would answer the bell - they didn't). Avoid sitting on one of the few benches to have a snack – no eating or drinking is allowed – and photographs cannot be taken.

Indeed, it most certainly is not a nature reserve: like most Jewish cemeteries, there are few trees and little grass, any hedges that are there mostly surround family plots (paths of pebbles tend to separate the graves). It is mostly immaculately kept and most inscriptions are decipherable. Only a few of the much older headstones and monuments have fallen or are broken.

Through the gate one comes to the memorial for the Jewish service personnel who died in the Second World War and in that area are the graves of most recent years and decades – although some of these can still be found in the older parts of the cemetery. They stand in well-ordered ranks. Most are the same height, and are mostly simple broad headstones on a base. With a flat terrain, none block the view of others that are way back. Like the older memorials, almost invariably there is a Hebrew inscription together with one in English and a Star of David engraved or surmounting the stone. Some also list birth and death dates in the conventional way, while adding those in the Jewish calendar.

Tributes are frequently paid to a record of public service, both to the Jewish and the wider community. On the modern headstones, in particular, mention is made of many of the bereaved – often by name – so that children, brothers and sisters, in-laws, grandchildren and often great-grandchildren are remembered. Grandchildren and great-grandchildren have often had a small memorial of their own placed on the base.

As one walks southwards, one goes further into the older part of the cemetery. Here the memorials are higher, more flamboyant but, even for the most distinguished, have nothing of the ostentation that one finds in so many of the cemeteries in this book, such as Highgate, West Norwood and Nunhead.

The old memorials have, of course, weathered in varying degrees (though this is not always the case – indeed, many looked as if they had just been erected). Among the newer ones there is almost a riot of black and white marble and granite. On the older graves there are broken columns, canopies (the Edgar family tomb is the most impressive), urns draped and undraped, scrolls, small obelisks, and even a small cenotaph.

What is interesting is that the *crème de la crème* of Jewish society has been laid to rest in a cemetery in the middle of such an unprepossessing area. There are numerous knights, baronets, fellows of the Royal Academy, business people, rabbis – including the Chief Rabbi Sir Isaac Brody (1895–1979) – and others.

There are numerous Rothschilds, including Baron Meyer Amschiel de Rothschild (1818–1874). He was the son of the founder of the British branch of the banking dynasty, and is buried with his cousin and wife, Juliana (died aged 46 in 1877) and their daughter, Hannah (1851–1890). Hannah is remembered by a plaque on their marble plot. However, she also has her own very similar plot next door. She died of typhoid at Dalmeny Castle, home of the Earl of Rosebery, whom she had married. Her death shattered him and while he attained the premiership, his rule was undistinguished and the rest of his 30 years he spent rudderless in the political wilderness. She was, her inscription says, 'The child of many hopes, the woman of rich fulfilment'. She was also said to be the richest woman in Britain.

There are several family plots surrounded by a marble ledge mounted on pillars. Notable among these is that for the Samuel family, later the Viscounts Bearsted, and the first three of that title are buried here with their wives. One here is Marcus Samuel (1853–1927), sometime Lord Mayor of London and founder of what was Shell Transport and Trading Company. On the plot, too, is a broken column, a memorial to a son, Gerald Samuel, who died, aged 31 in 1917, at the Battle of Messines.

Barnett 'Barney' Barnato (1851–1897), the Whitechapel-born financier who became a diamond magnate in South Africa, died when he went overboard on a voyage home. There were claims made of suicide but his body was recovered to lie with his relatives, Joel, Isaacs and Barnato, in their identical red granite, rounded table tombs enclosed in a family plot.

Barnato is not the only businessman buried here. Arnold (later Lord) Weinstock (1924–2002), the industrialist who created GEC (to be renamed Marconi), has a headstone of simple white marble next to the one in black marble of his son Simon (1952–1996), businessman and fellow race horse owner. Sir Jack Cohen (1898–1979), the East End market trader who created Tesco, has a magnificent, large, simple but uncluttered marble headstone with a grey marble base.

I counted 15 graves of the Franklin family whose most distinguished and best known member, Rosalind Franklin (1920–1958), has the most modest of graves: a flat white stone. Her work led to the discovery of the DNA double helix and her inscription refers to her work on viruses that 'remain of lasting benefit to mankind'. She lies with her parents, grandparents and great-grandparents. Some distance away rests her great uncle Herbert (later Lord) Samuel (1870–1963), the first practising Jew to serve in a British Cabinet, Leader of the Liberal Party and, in 1951, the first British politician to deliver a party political broadcast on television.

Gerald Reitlinger (1900–1978), noted historian of the Holocaust, also rests here under a simple, flat stone of white marble, overshadowed by the memorials to other members of his family.

The divisions within Judaism can be observed by these two adjoining cemeteries. Some cemeteries (not either of these, though) are reserved for the Sephardim (those Jews whose origins lie in the Iberian Peninsula) and the Ashkenazim (those Jews who originate from Eastern Europe and Russia), or have separate sections in each set aside for those from these communities. These differences are further divided by an attachment to either the United or Liberal Synagogues. The divisions between the Orthodox United and the Liberal and Reform Synagogues can be characterised by their differing attitudes toward female clergy, same sex ceremonies, understandings of who is Jewish and who is not – the United Synagogue does not accept conversions – attitude towards the Torah, and general observance.

The United Cemetery is divided by a high wall from the Liberal Synagogue Cemetery and there is no gate between the two. The visitor must leave the older cemetery and walk 10 minutes to find its newer mate down a narrow road next to a fire station. It is more than just a wall that separates the Jews of two very different traditions. The Liberal Synagogue is a much smaller cemetery without any large memorials, but with some beautifully kept graves. The overwhelming impression is of a sea of white. At the point where the lanes part, one comes first to the small Holocaust memorial that was erected in 1957.

There are far fewer well known people buried here than next door but one can find the impresario Bernard (later Lord) Delfont (1909–1994), the former cabinet minister Harold (later Lord) Lever (1914–1995), and the singer Sylvia Handel Samuel (1914–1998), whose voice, her inscription tells us, was loved by millions. Also here, too, is the American-born pianist, civil rights campaigner Hephibah *[sic]* Menuhin Hauser (1920–1981). She was the violinist Yehudi Menuhin's sister. Her second husband, the Austrian sociologist Richard Hauser (1911–1990), with whom she collaborated, rests next to her.

As in the United Cemetery, the plight and flight of the Jews is much in evidence. In the place for the burial of ashes – the United Cemetery has none as the Orthodox Jewry does not accept cremation – there are one or two memorials for family members who died in the Holocaust. But names sometimes betoken foreign birth and headstones, too, refer to foreign birthplaces, while one like that of Leopold Apelbaum (1881–1962) speaks volumes of history, international and personal, with the words 'Briesen-Berlin-London'.

Note: Adjoining the United and Liberal Synagogue Cemeteries is the New Willesden municipal cemetery. This is not to be confused with Paddington (Willesden Lane) Cemetery (see note on page 2).

Getting there
Dollis Hill tube station

Friends' association
No

Tours
No

Take a break
There are a large numbers of cheap takeaways that even those with the least fastidious palate might wish to avoid

Something else to see
BPS Shri Swaminarayan Temple, 105–199 Brentfield Road NW10

West Norwood (South Metropolitan) Cemetery

Norwood Road SE27

A visitor to West Norwood Cemetery may well wonder what it was like before the depredations that took place after Lambeth Council's compulsory purchase in 1965. Before that the signs had augured well – the rights of existing grave owners had been maintained, the legislation that established the cemetery and dictated how it should be run was never repealed, offering apparent protection. Within 13 years it was included within a conservation area and three years later the imposing entrance arch, gates, railings and 44 monuments were listed (seven as Grade II*, the remainder Grade II and another 21 monuments have since been listed).

However, this seems to not have mattered much to its municipal owners whose policies of 'lawn conservation' caused at least 10,000 monuments to be removed with no proper records kept of the positions of graves or which monuments had been destroyed, while the rights of grave owners were ignored. In addition, more than 1,000 private graves were resold for new burials.

The Chancellor of the Diocese of Southwark, which has responsibility for the 80% of the cemetery that is consecrated, stepped in and in 1991 Lambeth's vandalism was stopped. However, this was not before two listed monuments had disappeared and several others had been badly damaged. In 1994, the Consistory Court said that the lawn conversions and the reselling of the plots had been illegal.

Even allowing for the official vandalism and Lambeth's efforts to make some amends – by restoring and repairing many of the listed monuments, carrying out a landscape management survey, and renovating boundary walls and railings – the effect of the worst of what happened is difficult to imagine as this still looks like what it was intended to be: one of the Magnificent Seven, a startling example of Victorian and Edwardian funerary architecture and design in the Greek Revival style, a necropolis worthy of the name.

West Norwood has some of the finest collection of sepulchral monuments in London, although Kensal Green (see page 82) has the largest and most significant collection. West Norwood features 69 Grade II and Grade II* buildings and structures, including a Greek section that has 18 listed mausoleums and monuments. Its cultural, historical and architectural value, which was first recognised with that conservation area status 45 years ago, has been further acknowledged by English Heritage, who placed it on the National Register of Historic Parks and Gardens. By 2000, there had been 164,000 burials in 42,000 plots, and 34,000 cremations.

The impression that this cemetery gives now is one for which it has always been valued, and one that its designers envisaged. That impression is no more apparent than when approaching the main entrance. The entrance arch, by the architect Sir William Tite (1798–1873), bears the arms of the diocese of Winchester (which oversaw the place until that task passed, via the diocese of Rochester, to the diocese of Southwark in 1905) and the archdiocese of Canterbury. Above the pedestrian entrance is a carved crown and a scroll, inscribed, 'Deus Deo' and, on the inner side, '1837'.

West Norwood was the second of the large commercial, non-denominational cemeteries to be opened, following Kensal Green's creation in 1833. Like that cemetery and those that followed, it was set in a rural area distant from the growing capital. It was designed by Tite, who was a director of the cemetery company (he also landscaped Brookwood Cemetery) and put faith in his creation by having himself interred here. Apart from the walls, railings and entrance, all that we have now of Tite's work is his Gothic monument for the banker and author James Gilbart (1794–1863).

The cemetery was built on the site of the ancient Great North Wood, from which Norwood took its name. Tree clearing was, of course, extensive, but a number remained as part of the original landscaping. In 2005, a tree survey of the cemetery identified one oak that is believed to date from 1540–1640. Fourteen more oaks, a maple and an ash tree were identified as having been there when the cemetery was laid out.

The site originally included two Gothic chapels at the crest of the hill, which dominated the local landscape. The Bishop of Winchester consecrated the cemetery in the year it opened. There were 42 acres, with a west-facing Anglican chapel that looked like a small cathedral, its entrance flanked with two octagonal towers, and cloisters spanning over the Anglican catacombs. The chapel was demolished as a result of wartime bombing. To the north was a Dissenters' chapel, with its north entrance flanked by cloisters set over its unconsecrated catacombs. The catacombs together could hold 3,500 coffins. There was also a columbarium (a public place for the storage of cremated remains).

In 1842, the Greek necropolis was added when four wealthy Greek merchants took a lease on part of the unconsecrated area. Over the next 47 years more land was taken, creating an enclosure of 25,000 square feet. Stephen Ralli (1829–1902), head of Ralli Brothers, the foremost Anglo-Greek merchants in London, built the Grade II* listed St Stephen's Chapel in Bath stone, in what was then the unusual Greek Revival style. It was constructed to commemorate his son Augustus, who died of rheumatic fever when at Eton in 1872 aged 15. Ralli, his wife Marietta (1838–1922) and other relatives rest there. The pediment over the entrance contains, in Greek, the words: 'For the trumpet shall sound and the dead shall rise'.

The wealth of the community buried here is spoken for by the tombs and statuary. Much of it is in the neoclassical style, which, if anything, outdoes even the place that has given it a home. The family mausoleum of Peter Padia Ralli (1837–1868) is also Grade II* listed, while another 16 monuments are Grade II listed. Several of these belong to other members of the extended Ralli family, which is appropriate as an earlier generation had brought the necropolis into being. When the Greek section here was full, burials began to take place at Hendon (see And elsewhere..., page 144).

The cemetery is a relatively easy place to walk about; most of the notable graves are either on the edge of the winding roads and small paths that link them or are set not too far back. The Greek section is easy to walk around.

The visitor has barely passed beneath the entrance arch and set out before coming to an array of monuments, each apparently competing with the one next to it or across the path. One of the first to see is Edmund Distin Maddick's (1857–1939) impressive, if dreary, modernist mausoleum in Portland stone, on the left of the main path to the left of the cemetery office. It looks like a small house. Maddick trained at St Thomas' Hospital, London and became a Royal Navy surgeon, and surgeon to the Italian Hospital in London, in which capacity he entertained the Italian monarch and became a knight of the Italian Crown for his troubles. A rich man, he built the Scala Theatre in London where early colour films were shown. He had planned that his family should rest with him, but such was the state of his family life that he has the place all to himself.

Before moving further into the cemetery, look across the way to the resting place of someone with an arguably less benevolent legacy for the human race than that of his neighbour – Sir Hiram Stevens Maxim (1840–1916). He invented the lightweight, rapid-firing automatic machine gun that bears his name. While he also invented the electric filament lamp, Maxim, born in the USA, who took British nationality, also invented new explosives.

Perhaps because of it being the second of the Magnificent Seven, West Norwood attracted many eminent people who wished to be buried here; consequently it has monuments, which, it has been said, compare favourably with those in St Paul's Cathedral or even Westminster Abbey. Thus, Maddick, Maxim and Tite are far from being alone in this spectral *Who's Who*. There are sportsmen, inventors, engineers, architects, artists, entertainers and doctors. There are also others, such as the ballet dancer, Katti Lanner (1829–1908) and Baron Paul Julius de Reuter (1816–1899), whose pink granite monument, topped by an urn, is maintained by the news agency that bears his name. Mrs Isabella Beaton (1836–1865), who died in childbirth, rests under the original base of the family grave. Above is a more recent modest headstone for when, in the 1930s, the headstone fell into disrepair, it was replaced by what we see now courtesy of her two surviving children.

Thanks to the detective work of Paul Graham (revealed in his Friends' publication, *The Dickens Connection*) we know that 39 people with connections to Charles Dickens are buried here. These include George Cattermole (1800–1868), illustrator of *Barnaby Rudge* and *The Old Curiosity Shop*; Theodore Watts-Dunton (1832–1914), friend of Algernon Swinburne, novelist and poetic eulogist of Dickens; John Henry Barrow (1796–1858), a journalist who employed the young Dickens as a reporter in the gallery of the House of Commons; and Richard John Smith (1786–1855), an actor who played Scrooge and Bill Sikes, among others, on stage.

The multiplicity of non-British sounding names on graves of some age attests to the long history of the area as a place of settlement for those from overseas. This must be the only burial place where one can find a Virtue and a Modesty or where one such as DA Herschell, who died at the age of 80 in 1904 proclaims himself 'a Jew by birth, a Christian by grace'. It is finely symbolic of the variety of humankind who rest within these walls.

Getting there
West Norwood Rail Station

Friends' association
Yes

Tours
Yes

Take a break
O Girasol, 382a Norwood Road SE27

Something else to see
St Luke's Church, Norwood High Street SE27

And elsewhere...

Brockley and Ladywell Cemetery
Brockley Road SE4

Students of Victorian tragedy with a taste for melodramatic flourish might well want to visit this cemetery for the grave of Jane Clouson, who rests beneath a well-preserved, tall, upright plinth, with a pleading waif on top. The inscription calls her 'a motherless girl, who was murdered in Kidbrooke Lane Eltham aged 17 in 1871'. It then adds: 'Her last words were, "Oh, let me die"'. It is also said (but not on the memorial) that she said 'Edmund Pook'. It is believed that she had arranged to meet her former lover of that name, believing he would marry her after she had been dismissed from her job as servant/maid to his father Ebenezer Pook, a print works owner, because of her relationship with the son. She was brutally murdered with a hammer and was found to be pregnant (a fact that she and Edmund had known). Her funeral attracted thousands. Pook was tried for her murder but, despite much evidence against him, was acquitted. The public delivered its own verdict by both forcing the Pooks to leave their home and subscribing to raise the memorial.

Getting there: Croft Park, Ladywell and Brockley rail stations

East Sheen Cemetery
Sheen Road TW10

Those seeking unusual monuments could not do better than visiting this small cemetery, which is entered along an avenue of plane trees. The grave of William Rennie-O'Mahony, who died of war wounds when he was 34 in 1928, has what is, one assumes, an African member of the King's African Rifles (which, presumably, Williams was not) sitting defiantly, a rifle across one knee, in the regimental battle dress. Puttees cover naked legs as he wears some kind of kilt or short trousers. Here, too, is the tomb of coal mine owners, the Lancaster family. An immense, mourning bronze angel, dramatically prostrate, holds one arm across the tomb, while her wings drape behind. The actors Roy Kinnear (1934–1988) and Fulton Mackay (1922–1987), who may well have shared a stage or a TV programme, also share the cemetery.

Getting there: Richmond tube and rail stations

Great Northern Cemetery (New Southgate)
Brunswick Park Road N11

This cemetery is unusual for the variety of groups of people who are buried here. In the late 1900s, the Quakers erected a striking obelisk with the intention that members of the Society of Friends were to be buried nearby. Alas, it has been sadly stripped of its bronze plaques and is now surrounded by tombs. Not far away is a stone slab with a German inscription to mark the 51 German civilians who died at Alexandra Palace during the First World War. In the late 1960s, the Hendon Reform Synagogue and Columbarium were built here and nearby is a section for Greek Orthodox burials. There is also a Caribbean area, created with special sandy soil to allow the West Indian custom of having the grave filled in by members of the bereaved family. Not to be outdone, Catholics have a statute of the Virgin Mary, supported on five Doric columns, who watches over all.

The cemetery's earliest communal grave contains the remains taken from the Savoy Chapel in the Strand after the devastating fire in 1864. Many of them were Hanoverian courtiers, as the names on the covering slabs testify. There are also more than two dozen coffins and nearly 200 boxes of remains reinterred from St Michael Bassishaw. This was a Wren church that was demolished in 1899 after its foundations became insecure when the city's sanitary authorities were charged with clearing the crypt of human remains. Other exhumed remains are from the burial ground of the tiny 13th century St Mary Mountshaw, which burned down in the Great Fire of 1666. They came here when Queen Victoria Street was being constructed. The remains from the churchyard of St Mary-le-Savoy, the German Lutheran Church, were reburied here after the church, school and other buildings were replaced by the Crown on another site under an Act of Parliament when the Thames Embankment was built in 1870.

The Great Northern is also home to 'the most sacred site in the West'. This is the walled garden, which surrounds the marble column, surmounted by a globe on which sits a golden eagle. This marks the final resting place of Shogi Effendi (1896–1957) who died in London. He was the leader of the *Baha'i* faith and grandson of the founder of the faith.

Getting there: Arnos Grove tube and New Southgate rail stations

Greenwich Cemetery
Well Hall Road SE9

This cemetery of this modest south London suburb may not be able to boast of remarkable tombs or many notable residents. However, a panorama stretches below this hillside site that includes St Paul's Cathedral, the City, Canary Wharf and Crystal Palace. Its other noteworthy fact is the poignant section set aside for children and the one reserved for Norwegians who died in England as refugees during the Second World War.

Getting there: Eltham rail station

Gunnersbury Cemetery
Gunnersbury Avenue W3

While this cemetery does have a large number of notable people buried here – as diverse as the film director Sir Carol Reed (1906–1976) and the spy Greville Wynn (1919–1990) – it is not the most attractive of places or one to seek unusual monuments. That is, with one exception and it is that which makes it worth a visit. This is the great, imposing, black, marble obelisk dedicated in 1976. The words on the monument itself tell its own story: 'In remembrance of 14,500 Polish prisoners of war who disappeared in 1940 from camps at Kozielsk, Starobielsk and Ostaszkow of whom 4,500 were later identified in mass graves at Katyn near Smolensk'. And, added later are the words: 'This casket contains soil from their grave. Murdered by the Soviet secret police on Stalin's orders 1940. The soil hereunder came from their graveyard in 1990. As finally admitted in April 1990 by the USSR after 50 years shameful denial of the truth'.

In the (Catholic) southern part of the cemetery there are some Polish tombs and others from Eastern Europe, including Prince Vsevolod Ivanovich (1914–1973), great-great grandson of Tsar Nicholas I and a cousin of the murdered last Tsar, Nicholas II. He was the last surviving member of the Russian royal family to have been born in that country.

Getting there: Acton town tube and Gunnersbury tube and rail stations

Hendon Cemetery
Holder's Hill Road NW7

With the Egyptian entrance of Abney Park (see page 18), Hendon's entrance must rank as one of the most imposing but also the most eclectic of entrances. Large, engraved Gothic letters on the left of the main gate announce it. This is part of a part mock Tudor and part pseudo-Gothic frontage, with Elizabethan chimneys. Once through the gate, the busy suburban roads that surround these 40 acres fall away to peaceful, almost rural grounds, where bird song, not the hum of traffic, accompanies the visitor in walks past mature trees and hedges. A stream, crossed by small bridges, running along the eastern side, enhances this rusticity.

So, apart from its rural aspect, Hendon's interest is the number of people of foreign origin who rest here. Apart from many Chinese and Eastern European names, there are others from Spain and Vietnam. There are two, fairly unremarkable Muslim sections (the 'old' and the 'new'), but it is the Greek and Japanese sections that are worth visiting.

The Japanese section, provided by the Japanese Residents Association (UK) seems, literally, alien to its surroundings, as if this had been transplanted from a quiet park in Tokyo. Graves, with stones set flat into the ground within a pavement surround, are reached past two stone columns with receptacles on top for lamps. On either side stand wooden notice boards on stilts and at the top of the section a mounted plaque that says, touchingly, 'In memory of our friends who made their lives here'. In the middle is a small, stepped cenotaph. This is a quiet, moving spot.

By contrast, the Greek section is announced by the number of Greek graves one finds elsewhere in the cemetery. It is approached through a metal gate and surrounded by a hedge, a large plot with an array of marble tombs, memorials and mausoleums. Most striking among these belong to the Lemos family and Erato Pittalis (1826–1904) whose splendid white bust stands next to that of her (unnamed) husband. There are two fine sarcophagi, one decorated with mosaics. There is also a large, shining white mausoleum, engraved only with the name Lord Marks (1920–1968). The local authority knew nothing about this Michael Marks. The better-known Lord (Simon) Marks was the former head of Marks and Spencer and himself son of another (but unennobled) Michael Marks, the co-founder of the company. But this is he: the second Lord Marks converted to the Greek Orthodox faith when he married his fifth wife.

Also to be found in the cemetery are the graves of Joseph Havelock Wilson (1859–1929), founder of the National Sailors' and Firemen's Union and twice Liberal MP for Middlesbrough and once for South Shields; and Edwin Mullins (1848–1907), the sculptor.

Getting there: Mill Hill East tube

Huguenot Cemetery
East Hill SW18

Opened in about 1687 as a burial ground for the French Church that once stood opposite the Wandsworth parish church All Saints, this historic place is also known as Mount Nod. It is a small, attractive and tree-shaded spot, with walls topped by spikes and railings along one boundary. It contains five Grade II listed tombs.

The Huguenot refugees rest here. They settled in Wandsworth when 20,000 of them fled their native France following the Revocation of the Edict of Nantes in 1685, which had granted equality to Protestants with a degree of religious freedom and toleration. The cemetery was enlarged in 1700 and

Who's buried where

This is a highly selective list of people, famous and infamous, significant and interesting, who are buried in the cemeteries and burial places featured in the main section. Some of those mentioned in the main entries are given here, but most are noted for the first time.

Abney Park Cemetery

Rev Andrew Buzzacott (1829–1881). Congregational minister and secretary of the Anti-Slavery Society.

Joseph Cornfield (1809–1888). The Reformers' Memorial, which he had erected at Kensal Green, commemorates the 85 'men and women who have generously given their time and means to improve the conditions and enlarge the happiness of all classes'.

Mary Hillum (1759–1864). According to her gravestone, she 'died in the same house she was born, scarcely ever slept out of the house in the whole of her life, never travelled by omnibus or railway, and was never more than 15 minutes from her house'.

John Remington Mills (1798–1879). A millionaire before he inherited his brother's fortune that made him one of the wealthiest commoners in the country, he was a Congregationalist and philanthropist.

Sir Hugh Owen (1804–1881). Philanthropist who founded the University College of Wales, Aberystwyth.

Rev Andrew Reed (1787–1862). Founder of the Royal Hospital for Incurables.

Henry Vincent (1813–1878). Chartist. His imprisonment in 1839 led to rioting. Later, he became a lecturer in England and America.

Brompton Cemetery

Sir Squire Bancroft (1841–1926). Actor-manager who introduced the drawing room comedy to London's theatre.

Charles Collins (1828–1873). Novelist and Pre-Raphaelite painter, brother of the novelist Wilkie Collins and Charles Dickens' son-in-law.

Sir Samuel Cunard (1787–1865). Born in America, he founded the shipping line that bore his name.

John Jackson (1769–1845). 'Gentleman Jim' Jackson, the boxing champion of England from 1795 to 1803.

Constant Lambert (1905–1951). Composer.

Samuel Smiles (1812–1904). Journalist, writer and author of *Self Help*.

Brandon Thomas (1850–1914). Playwright who wrote *Charlie's Aunt*.

Sir Andrew Waugh (1810–1878). Astronomer and surveyor-general in northern India. He surveyed and named Mount Everest after his former colleague Sir George Everest.

Bunhill Fields Burial Ground

Thomas Hardy (1752–1832). A boot maker in Piccadilly who was also a radical politician, which led him to be tried for high treason in 1794 for advocating parliamentary reform. He was acquitted.

Hanserd Knollys (1599–1691). Held several positions in Cromwell's governments.

Thomas Newcomen (1663–1729). Inventor of the first steam engine suitable for industrial use.

Daniel Quare (1648–1724). Watchmaker who invented the repeating watch. His clock for William III required winding only once a year.

Isaac Watts (1674–1748). Hymn writer whose works include 'O God, Our Help in Ages Past'.

City of London Cemetery

George Foote (1850–1915). Leading Victorian secularist and first editor of *The Freethinker*, who was imprisoned for blasphemy in 1882.

Benjamin Gardener (1865–1948). Labour MP for West Ham from 1923 to 1945.

George Micklewright (1817–1876). Conservationist, who worked with others to ensure that Epping Forest was not developed.

John Joseph Sims (1835–1881). Won the VC during the Crimean War for saving wounded comrades when under heavy fire. He received the medal personally from Queen Victoria. Died in the workhouse and was originally buried in an unmarked grave.

Rev Thomas Bowman Stephenson (1839–1912). Methodist clergyman and founder of the National Children's Home and Orphanage (now Action for Children).

East Finchley (St Marylebone) Cemetery

Henry Walter Bates (1825–1892). Naturalist and explorer, who gave the scientific explanation of mimicry in animals. He left England in 1842 with Alfred Russell Wallace to explore and collect insects in the Amazon basin. He spent 11 years in Amazonia amassing large collections of insects that were sent back to museums and collectors in Europe.

Sir Edmund Grosse (1849–1928). Librarian to the House of Lords and author of *Father and Son*.

Quintin Hogg (1845–1903). Tea and sugar trader. At the age of 37 he founded the Young Men's Christian Institute, which later became the Regent Street Polytechnic and the London Polytechnic and is now the University of Westminster.

Matilda Verne (1865–1936). Pianist and piano teacher to the Queen Mother.

Finchley (St Pancras and Islington) Cemetery

Cora Crippen (1875–1910). Actress wife of Dr Harvey Crippen, whom he murdered.

Sir Eugene Goossens (1893–1962). Violinist and conductor, born in England, the son and grandson of noted musicians. He was ruined when he resigned his positions in 1956 in disgrace, having been found guilty of possessing pornography after he had an affair with Rosaleen Norton, the so-called 'Witch of King's Cross', with whom he shared a taste for the occult and the erotic.

Ford Maddox-Brown (1821–1893). Pre-Raphaelite painter and associate of William Morris.

Robert Morrell (1823–1912). Through his Sunday League, he secured the opening of national museums on Sundays.

Mary Shepherd (died 1989). Resident in playwright Alan Bennett's London front garden, who gave rise to his *Lady in the Van*.

Hampstead Cemetery

Lajos Biro (1880–1948). Born in Hungary, where he was at one time foreign minister, he fled first to Vienna and then ended up in Hollywood. There he collaborated on the screenplays of, among other films, *The Private Life of Henry VIII*, *Catherine the Great*, *The Scarlet Pimpernel*, *The Four Feathers* and *The Thief of Bagdad*.

Clive Brook (1887–1976). For 40 years he was a leading stage and screen actor, who starred twice as Sherlock Holmes (1929 and 1932) and was in *Shanghai Express* with Marlene Dietrich in 1932.

Ann Dudin Brown (1823–1917). The daughter of a prosperous wharfinger and granary keeper, her donation of £10,000 helped to found Westfield College to advance the cause of higher education for women. After her parents died in 1855, she had no permanent home but lived in a succession of luxury hotels.

Peggy Duff (1910–1981). Described in a *Times* obituary as 'a born campaigner', Duff was the organiser of the first Aldermaston March and was for seven years general secretary of the Campaign for Nuclear Disarmament. From there she went to a similar post with the International Confederation for Disarmament and Peace. She was a Camden councillor for 15 years.

David Higham (died aged 82 in 1978). Literary agent and founder of the literary agency that still bears his name, and novelist. He created the award for fiction that bears his name, and represented, among others, Malcolm Muggeridge, John Braine, Anthony Powell and Dylan Thomas.

Sir Bernard Lima (1885–1919). Born in Brazil, an obituary said that work was his one interest in life. This was a tendency that saw him, only in his 20s, controlling and successfully running the *Leeds Mercury* and the *Glasgow Daily Record* and later become chairman of the *Daily Mirror* and the *Sunday Pictorial*. He was knighted for his wartime work for the Ministry of Information, he was a captain in the Canada Army and was one of the millions of victims of the post-war Spanish Flu epidemic.

David Morgan (died 1937). A pioneer of radiology, but his work so badly damaged his hands that he gave it up.

Arthur Prince (1881–1948). A ventriloquist known as 'the Master', he was the first to perfect drinking and talking at the same time. He took part in the first Royal Command Performance and he toured Australia and the United States. His dummy, Jim, is buried with him.

Sir Charles Wyndham (1837–1919). Born Charles Culverwell in Liverpool and the son of a doctor, he worked as an army surgeon during the American Civil War at the battles of Chancellorsville, Fredericksburg and Gettysburg. He returned to England and became the most famous actor-manager of his time, building the New Theatre (now the Albery) and the theatre that bears his name

Highgate (St James) Cemetery

William Betty (1791–1874). A child actor whose debut at Covent Garden when he was 13 (at 50 guineas a night for 12 performances), had the police controlling the crowds.

Jacob Bronowski (1908–1974). Scientist and broadcaster who presented the television series, *The Ascent of Man*.

Catherine Dickens (1815–1870). The long-suffering wife of Charles.

William Foyle (1885–1963). In 1903, he founded the bookshop with his brother Gilbert in Charing Cross Road, which is still run by the family.

Anna Mahler (1904–1988). Daughter of the composer, she was an award-winning sculptor. The memorial on her grave is a copy of an original statue now owned by her family.

Sir Sidney Nolan (1917–1992). Born in Melbourne, he is one of the pre-eminent artists of the 20th century who is best known for his Australian landscapes and his series on the outlaw Ned Kelly.

Joseph Payne (1808–1878). The first professor of education in England.

Peter Robinson (1804–1874). Founder of the store in Oxford Street that bears his name.

Herbert Spencer (1820–1903). Philosopher and sociologist, he coined the term 'survival of the fittest' and the modern use of the word 'evolution'.

Anna Swanwick (1813–1899). A writer and promoter of the cause of women's higher education, she was president of Bedford College and a founder of Girton College, Cambridge, and Somerville Hall, Oxford.

Kensal Green (All Souls) Cemetery

William Henry Ainsworth (1805–1882). Novelist, who, at one time, lived at nearby Kensal Lodge where Charles Dickens and William Makepeace Thackeray were among his guests.

William Babbage (1791–1871). Mathematician who was the first to construct a correct logarithm table and whose calculating table contained the principles of the modern computer.

Thomas Barnes (1785–1841). Editor of *The Times* when its strong advocacy of the 1832 Reform Bill earned it the title, 'The Thunderer'.

Marigold Frances Churchill (1818–1921). Daughter of Sir Winston and Lady Clementine Churchill.

Isabella Glyn (1823–1889). The theatrical name (in fact, her maiden name) of Isabella Dallas, a leading tragic actress.

Frances ('Fanny') Anne Kemble (1809–1893). One of the most noted actresses of her day who played most of the great Shakespearean roles. She is less known for her advocacy of the abolitionist cause in the USA where her husband owned hundreds of slaves on his family's Southern plantations.

Viscount Strangford (1818–1875). Conservative MP and a member of Disraeli's grouping, Young England. It is believed that the Disraeli based the hero of Coningsby on him. He took part in the last duel to be fought in England in 1852.

Anthony Trollope (1815–1882). Novelist and author of the 'Barsetshire' series of novels.

Louisa Twining (1829–1912). Social reformer in the field of workhouses and the treatment of paupers, she collaborated with Florence Nightingale in sending trained nurses into the homes of the poor.

Sir Leslie Ward (1851–1922). Caricaturist, whose *nom de crayon*, 'Spy', was used during the 38 years he worked for *Vanity Fair* to produce 1,325 caricatures – some of the originals now in the National Gallery – which portrayed those in the Church, politics, the military and the arts.

Liberal Jewish Synagogue

Sir Isaac Shoenberg (1880–1963). Russian-born electronic engineer who designed and installed the earliest wireless stations in Russia. He emigrated to the UK, worked for Marconi and later with the Columbia Graphaphone Company (which merged with EMI). He contributed much to the development of television.

Sir Andrew Shonfield (1917–1981). Journalist, economist, Reith lecturer (1972) and one-time director of the Royal Institute of International Affairs.

Moravian Burial Ground

Peter Boehler (1712–1775). German-born evangelist, bishop and missionary to Pennsylvania and one-time superintendent of the church in England.

John Cennick (1718–1755). Former Methodist who became a Moravian evangelist (he helped establish over 40 churches in England and Ireland) and hymn writer.

Nunhead (All Saints) Cemetery

Robert Abel (1857–1936). English test cricketer. His 357 runs in 1899 remained a record until 1938.

Lavinia Bartlett (1806–1875). Baptist preacher who attracted large numbers at London's Metropolitan Tabernacle.

William Bennett (1820–1895). Poet and journalist, who assisted Gladstone in his campaign to become Liberal MP for Greenwich in 1868.

Sir Ernest Budge (1857–1934). Keeper of antiquities at the British Museum. As an archaeologist he undertook excavations in Mesopotamia and Egypt.

Charles Carpenter (1858–1938). A civil engineer who was a pioneer of chemical warfare in the First World War.

Peter Cunningham (1789–1864). Surgeon superintendent of convict ships to Australia.

Old St Pancras Churchyard

John Flaxman (1755–1826). Sculptor and first professor of sculpture to the Royal Academy.

William Jones (died 1836). When he was 'master of a respectable school in this parish' – Wellington House Classical and Commercial Academy – one of his pupils was Charles Dickens. Mr Creakle, the schoolmaster in *David Copperfield*, is thought to be based on him.

Capt John Mills (1727–1811). Survivor of the siege known as the Black Hole of Calcutta in 1756.

St John at Hampstead Old Churchyard and Additional Burial Ground

Sir Walter Besant (1836–1901). Essayist, playwright and novelist, his novels sold in their hundreds of thousands. He campaigned for the employment of middle class women, against sweatshops and for entertainment places for the working class. He was a prime mover in the creation of the Society of Authors.

Catherine Carswell (1878–1946). Glasgow-born book reviewer, novelist and biographer, her demythologising biography of Robert Burns was the subject of a hostile sermon in Glasgow Cathedral. She also wrote an affectionate portrait of DH Lawrence, whose talent she had been one of the first to recognise and who became her friend.

Cyril Joad (1891–1953). Writer, philosopher and broadcaster, who gained great national fame by his membership of BBC radio's *Brain's Trust* panel. A habitual fare dodger, his reputation was in ruins when he was found guilty of travelling without a train ticket.

Sir Herbert Beerbohm Tree (1853–1917). Actor-manager, who founded the Royal Academy of Dramatic Art and built Her Majesty's Theatre.

Evelyn Moore (1875–1941). Known by her maiden name as Evelyn Underhill, she was enormously influential as a writer on mysticism and spirituality – she published 39 books. She was also a conductor of retreats and a spiritual director.

Anton Walbrook (1869–1967). Born in Vienna, he was a star of stage and screen who acted in the films *Gaslight*, *The Life and Death of Colonel Blimp*, *The Red Shoes*, *Saint Joan* and the stage production of *Call Me Madam*.

St Mary's Roman Catholic Cemetery

Sir John Gatti (1872–1929). Born in Italy to a family who were prominent as London restaurateurs, theatre owners and entrepreneurs, he ran the theatre part of the business (owning the Adelphi and the Vaudeville) but also moved into electricity and the building of power stations. A Conservative, he served both as Lord Mayor of Westminster and chairman of the London County Council.

James Mann (1838–1899). Chamberlain to Pope Leo XIII.

Victoria Monks (1884–1927). Music hall artist who popularised the song, 'Won't You Come Home, Bill Bailey?'.

Sir Antony Panizzi (1797–1879). Italian-born principal librarian of the British Museum. It was through his efforts that the Reading Room was constructed.

Carlo Pellegrini (1839–1889). Italian-born caricaturist, who, as 'Ape', worked for *Vanity Fair* from 1869 until his death.

Tower Hamlets Cemetery

Alexander Hurley (1871–1913). Music hall performer and second husband of Marie Lloyd.

John 'White Hat' Willis (dates unknown). Original owner of the Cutty Sark and owner of the company that built it.

United Synagogue Cemetery

Sir Israel Brodie (1895–1979). Chief Rabbi of the United Congregations of the British Commonwealth, first president of the Zionist Federation of Australia, and the first Chief Rabbi to be knighted.

Joseph Herman Hertz (1872–1846). Brodie's predecessor as Chief Rabbi.

Sir Charles Clore (1904–1979). Businessman, owner of several shoe shop chains and one-time director of the Ritz Hotel, London.

Lord Duveen (1869–1939). Art dealer and benefactor of galleries and the British Museum.

Marc Tager (died 1988). A victim of the Lockerbie bombing.

Sir Julius Vogel (1835–1899). London-born eighth prime minister of New Zealand and the only practising Jew to hold that office in any country (except Israel).

West Norwood (South Metropolitan) Cemetery

William Roupell (1831–1909). Forger and Liberal MP, who in less than a decade squandered and gambled away £184,000 and then served 14 years penal servitude.

Dr William Marsden (1796–1867). In 1818 he set up a small establishment in Hatton Garden to offer medical care to the poor, which became the Royal Free Hospital. His small treatment centre for cancer in Westminster is the Royal Marsden Hospital.

Thomas Cubitt (1788–1885), a speculative builder who laid out many of the streets and squares in Belgravia, Pimlico and Bloomsbury.

Maria Zambaco or Maria Cassavetti (1843–1914). She was an artists' model and an artist who designed medals exhibited at the Royal Academy. She was also the lover of Sir Edward Burne-Jones, despite their both being married.

Sir Henry Doulton (1820–1897). Turned the family pottery business into more artistic ware now known as Royal Doulton.

Charles Haddon Spurgeon (1834–1892). A great Baptist preacher, who founded Spurgeon's Orphanage (now Spurgeon's Homes) and the still existing Spurgeon's College for the training of Baptist ministers.

Sir Henry Tate (1819–1899). A Liverpool grocer whose business later became Tate & Lyle, who founded libraries and donated his collection of contemporary art to the nation in Tate Britain.

Symbols and what they mean

Cemeteries display a wide variety of funerary symbols that surmount graves and tombs or are carved into headstones.

The fashion for symbols has changed over the years. For much of the 19th century for Anglicans, but particularly for Nonconformists, anything that seemed reminiscent of Catholicism was avoided. Simple classical styles became associated with Protestantism.

However, symbols taken from the pagan world became very popular: the urn, the torch and the drape were borrowed from Rome and Greece. Nunhead and Highgate, in particular, are also known for their use of Egyptian motifs. Gothic decoration and lettering, and Celtic crosses, too, are to be found in the richness of sepulchral art. While a simple cross can also be found on Commonwealth War Commission graves (or the crescent or Star of David as appropriate), perhaps the stark simplicity of the uniform white headstone symbolises the equality of sacrifice.

Some symbols make direct reference to the deceased's occupation (as with hammers) or interests (as with horses) or worldly companions (as with dogs).

Whatever the symbol, they speak, often very expressively, about death, the immortality of the soul and the mortality of the body, and the individual who has died.

Anchor and/or rock and/or chain: Holding fast to the Christian faith. St Peter – Petrus – was the rock on which Christ said he would build his Church. The anchor may sometimes indicate a seafarer.

Angel and trumpet: Day of judgement.

Angels: Guardians of the dead and/or a comforter.

Bird (often a dove): Flying down with the Holy Spirit; flying up as the soul ascends; perched as above Noah's ark at the flood.

Book: Faith and the book of life.

Broken columns: Life cut short.

Broken or severed flower: A sign of early or sudden death (severed bud denotes the death of a child).

Butterfly: Resurrection.

Celtic cross: From ancient Celtic Christianity, where the central circle signifies eternity.

Cherubim: Hope and innocence.

Circle: Eternity.

Clasped hands: The hope of reunification after death; a loving bond.

Cross: Faith; Christianity (more properly, Christ's suffering and resurrection and thus a belief in the afterlife).

Cut flowers: Life cut short.

Dove: Peace and purity; the Holy Spirit ascending.

Draped urn: The soul having left the body (some claim that this is simply a sign of death), signifying mourning.

Extinguished torch: The absence of light and hence death.

Forget me not: Eternal memory.

Gate or arch: Gateway to heaven.

Heart: Love.

Hourglass: The passing of allotted time.

IHS: The first three letters in Greek of Jesus or (in popular belief but not historically accurate), in the Latinised version of the Greek, 'Jesus, Saviour of Man'.

Inverted torch: The snuffing out of life.

Ivy: Memory will never fade.

Lamp: The light of knowledge and truth.

Laurel wreath: Accolade to life's achievements.

Lily: Purity.

Lyre or harp: Recognition of musical talent.

Palm frond: The triumph of life over death through resurrection.

Rocks: St Peter as the rock on which the Church is built, or the rock of faith.

Rose: Innocence and goodness.

Set square and compasses: Masonic symbols.

Skull: Reminder of death.

Serpent: Ancient Egyptian symbol for life and death (where the tail is being swallowed, to make a circle, life eternal).

Three-stepped platform on which stands a cross: Faith, hope and charity.

Torch: The human being but also upright, human life; entwined by a snake, health; inverted, life extinguished.

Tree: The tree of life but also yew tree, evergreen (life after death); willow tree, mourning.

Urn: Death.

Weeping figures: Life cut short; bereavement.

Wheat: Gathered into new life (can denote death in later life).

Wreath: Victory in death.

10 things you (probably) didn't know about London's cemeteries

1. The only state-owned cemetery is Brompton Cemetery, which is run by the Royal Parks on behalf of the Department for Culture, Media and Sport.

2. The future novelist Thomas Hardy helped to clear graves from Old St Pancras Churchyard for the building of the Great Northern Railway when he was a young architect.

3. There are only three working coffin lifts in the country and two of them are in adjoining cemeteries in London – Kensal Green and St Mary's Roman Catholic Cemetery. (The third is in St George's Chapel, Windsor.)

4. The hymn writer Isaac Watts is buried in Bunhill Fields but there is a statue to him in Abbey Park Cemetery as he once lived in a house on the site now occupied by the cemetery.

5. St Mary's Roman Catholic Cemetery contains the graves of three spies and three members of the Bonaparte family.

6. Gunnersbury and Brompton Cemeteries are the last resting places of members of the exiled Russian royal family.

7. The two parts of Highgate Cemetery are joined by a tunnel, which allowed coffins to travel underground from the chapels in the West Cemetery for burial in the East Cemetery.

8. The Gardens of Peace Muslim Cemetery is the largest Muslim cemetery in Europe.

9. Catholics and others being taken for execution at Tyburn were offered a drink when they stopped at St Giles-in-the-Fields Church, and later were often taken back to be buried in the churchyard.

10. Three of Queen Victoria's close relatives are buried in Kensal Green Cemetery.

Reading list

One cannot truly really appreciate cemeteries only by reading about them, but visiting them for the purpose of writing a book – and, indeed, visiting them to seriously appreciate their history, architecture and those who lie within the gates – has been enhanced by the wide variety of written sources that are available.

Below is a list of books, guides and other publications I have read or consulted, indeed, in many cases, relied upon. Some have been invaluable during visits in helping me to see what there is to be seen. Other writers have so thoroughly done the groundwork, and I thank them for it. In particular, mention must be made of the many publications by Friends' associations. They often provide not only the standard and always informative general guide, but also sometimes specialist publications. With such loving scholarship, all visitors are in their debt. While the Friends of Tower Hamlets Cemetery are the exception in not publishing guides, the City of London Cemetery has no Friends' association, however the City of London Corporation has published David Lambert's excellent, well-illustrated but inexpensive guide.

Ackroyd P (2011) *London Under*. London: Chatto & Windus.

Anonymous (2010) *The Fetter Lane Congregation of the Moravian Church: A Brief History*.

Anonymous (No date) *A Guide to Hampstead Parish Church*.

Anonymous (No date) *Hampstead Parish Church: Additional Burial Ground – Tomb Trail*.

Anonymous (No date) *Hampstead Parish Church: Old Churchyard – Tomb Trail*.

Anonymous (No date) *St Pancras Old Church. A Church Guide*.

Anonymous (No date) *Saint Giles-in-The-Fields: Information for Visitors*.

Anonymous (No date) *St Giles-in-the-The-Fields: The Poets' Church*.

Anonymous (No date) *St Giles-in-the-Fields. A Short Guide and History*.

Anonymous (No date) *Bunhill Fields Burial Ground*. London: City of London Corporation.

Anonymous (1997) *Paths of Glory or A Select Alphabetical and Biographical List, Illustrated with Line Drawings of their Monuments, of Persons of Note Commemorated at The Cemetery of All Souls at Kensal Green*. London: Friends of Kensal Green Cemetery.

Arnold C (2007) *Necropolis: London and Its Dead*. London: Pocket Books.

Atkinson E (1998) *Church Tower and Row*. London: Hampstead Parish Church.

Banks FR (1990) *The New Penguin Guide to London* (11th edition). London: Penguin Books Ltd.

Beach D (2008) *London's Cemeteries*. London: Metro Publications.

Bianco D, Dudman J, Flanagan B, Graham P & White J (2007) *The South Metropolitan Cemetery, West Norwood: An Introductory Guide*. London: Friends of West Norwood Cemetery.

Brooks C (1989) *Mortal Remains: The History and Present State of the Victorian and Edwardian Cemetery*. London: Wheaton Publishers.

Colloms M & Weindling N (2000) *The Good Grave Guide to Hampstead Cemetery, Fortune Green*. London: Camden History Society.

Curl JS (2001) *The Victorian Celebration of Death*. Gloucestershire: Sutton Publishing Ltd.

Culbertson J & Randall T (1991) *Permanent Londoners: An Illustrated Guide to the Cemeteries of London*. London: Robson Books.

Eagle D & Stephens M (1992) *The Oxford Illustrated Literary Guide to Great Britain and Ireland* (2nd edition). Oxford: Oxford University Press.

Fenn CR & Slattery-Kavanagh J (2011) *West Norwood Cemetery's Greek Necropolis*. London: Friends of West Norwood Cemetery.

Flanagan B (1998) *West Norwood Cemetery. Music Hall*. London: Friends of West Norwood Cemetery.

Glinert E (2004) *The London Compendium: A Street-by-Street Exploration of the Hidden Metropolis*. London: Penguin Books Ltd.

Graham P (2005) *West Norwood Cemetery*. The Dickens Connection. London: Friends of West Norwood Cemetery.

Jenkins S (1999) *England's Thousand Best Churches*. London: Penguin Books Ltd.

Joyce P (1994) *A Guide to Abney Park Cemetery* (2nd edition). London: Abney Park Cemetery Trust.

Kerrigan M (1995) *Who Lies Where: A Guide to Famous Graves*. London: Fourth Estate.

Mellor H & Parsons B (2011) *London Cemeteries. An Illustrated Guide and Gazetteer* (5th edition). Stroud: The History Press.

Miller A (2012) *Pure*. London: Sceptre.

Nagdi S (2011) *Discovering Through Death – Beliefs and Practices*. Leicester: Muslim Burial Council of Leicestershire.

Oxford Dictionary of National Biography. Oxford: Oxford University Press.

Pateman J (2005) *In Highgate Cemetery*. London: Highgate Cemetery Ltd on behalf of The Friends of Highgate Cemetery.

Pevsner N (1952) *The Buildings of England. London. Vol 2*. London: Penguin Books Ltd.

Podmore C (1999) *The Moravian Cemetery 1728–1760*. Oxford: Oxford University Press.

Royal Parks, The (2002) *Brompton Cemetery*. London: The Royal Parks.

Rutherford S (2008) *The Victorian Cemetery*. Colchester: Shire Publishing.

Sinclair I (1997) *Lights Out for the Territory*. London: Granta Books.

Turpin J & Knight D (2011) *The Magnificent Seven: London's First Landscape Cemeteries*. Stroud: Amberley Publishing.

Weinreb B, Hibbert C, Keay J & Keay J (2008) *The Encyclopaedia of London* (revised 3rd edition). London: Macmillan.

Whitfield P (2006) *London: A Life in Maps*. London: The British Library.